I0558470

REFORM

A LIBERIAN DEVELOPMENT MANIFESTO

*How To Restructure and Reform An African Nation To Achieve
Political Stability, Assure Self-defense, Grow Its Economy, Provide
Opportunities, Improve Living Standards, and Create Wealth.*

NOROTOI GBONOI

Copyright © Year 2025.

All Rights Reserved by **Norotoi Gbonoi.**

No part of this publication may be reproduced in any form, or by any means, electronic or mechanical, including photocopying, recording, or any information browsing, storage, or retrieval system, without permission in writing from Norotoi Gbonoi.

ISBN

Hardcover: 978-1-969120-86-2

Paperback: 978-1-969120-85-5

For Ordinary Africans, Reformers, Activists, and those still fighting to liberate the continent of Africa.

About This Book

REFORM is a Liberian Development Manifesto that addresses how to reorganize, grow, and defend Liberia, thereby prospering its people. The primary focus of this guide is to reform the structure of government and overhaul its governing systems and practices in ways that will enable it to govern itself more effectively, improve the standard of living, and manage its affairs more efficiently.

As a small and vulnerable nation, Liberia faces serious security threats, economic exploitation, and external interference. Foreign control over key sectors, such as banking, defense, communications, and finance, is a clear example of external interference and dominance. Advice and consultations on developing and investing have also originated from external sources, often providing incorrect and misleading information.

Furthermore, Liberia's form of government and governing practices have not enabled it to adequately defend itself, manage its economy effectively, raise living standards, create wealth, participate in politics freely, and uphold the rule of law without outside interference. For several of these reasons, the current form of government needs to be changed. For that to happen, Liberians need to take on the responsibility of deciding and implementing what is good for them and pursuing what will make them whole.

The book opens with a case for reform and describes the expected changes. It calls for redefining the purpose and functions of the new Liberia in relation to the people's goals and aspirations.

The country needs to take a fresh look at how it protects itself and its interests, not just from enemies but also from competitors and even allies. How should it redevelop, invest in the future to prosper, and educate its people to rebuild and thrive? Because Liberia was founded as the home for slaves repatriated from the United States, the people operated under the beliefs and assumptions that they were Americans and that America was going to build the country for them, which was misleading and is not true today. Yet, those founding concepts and operational principles, which have not changed for nearly two centuries, continue to have profound implications on the nation and succeeding generations.

Second, it introduces readers to the concept of dividing and managing Liberia by District and replacing the current county's administrative system.

In the county administrative system, the president controls everything from Monrovia. In the District-City State System, based on land size and population, the residents, not the president, shall exercise those powers and authorities to make those decisions about problems that impact their communities.

In places around the world where people are free to make local decisions that affect their daily lives, independent of the president and national government, as proposed in the District-City Structure, they fare better than in places where the president controls everything from a distance.

In subsequent chapters, the current branches of government structures, operations, powers, and authorities are reformed and reorganized, reducing presidential powers and authorities and the cost of running the government. New roles and responsibilities are prescribed to the reformed entities. Plus, two branches of government are established through this process to manage the economy and provide robust oversight over all aspects of government and the state.

There are also discussions about creating large national companies and industries to produce goods and services for the domestic market, provide employment opportunities, and generate wealth for the people. The goal is to compete with foreign corporations and gain control of key industries where they currently hold a dominant position. This will be achieved through restructuring, transfers, mergers, and acquisitions of the current government ministries, agencies, and State-Owned Enterprises.

Finally, the book concludes with a list of general policy proposals that will complement the broader aspects of the reform in agriculture and food production, public finance, defense, security, law enforcement, investments, health, and education, promoting wealth creation and economic prosperity.

Although the book is more prescriptive of Liberia, it is practical and applicable to other third-world nations. With the right movements and reformers, the ideas in this book can serve as a plan for change in any African country. It can serve as a guide to help struggling nations grow, become stronger, and take control of their own future. Some solutions to Liberia's problems will be explicit or inherent in the issues discussed. But most of the strategies and maneuvers required to achieve these reforms and the overarching results in each country will depend on the specific situation, including training and consultations, which will be necessary, as outlined in this book.

Readers should view the ideas in this book as a testament to a defeated, dispossessed, yet courageous generation of Liberians attempting to rebuild an embattled nation and empower hopeless people with new methods, systems, and practices to address their problems. I hope that Liberians will view this book as the beginning of a serious discussion, debate, and planning of their national destiny, rather than waiting for a single president to show them the way or for foreigners to do it for them.

The ideas and systems in REFORM are borrowed from diverse sources through research, debates, suggestions, and listening, and combined to create a philosophy that makes Liberia unique and distinct. However, it was the questions and counterarguments of Liberians and friends that evolved and shaped the concepts in this book. Their contributions, as well as those of my editors, have been invaluable to the creation of this publication.

Norotoi Gbonoi

Author

Table of Contents

Introduction

Many of the solutions Liberia has used to solve its problems, or those currently imposed on it, have come from outsiders to the country's detriment. "Reform" is one of the few books written by a Liberian specifically for Liberia to reject that behavior and use our own ideas to solve our problems.

This exercise began in 1990, when I sought refuge during the Civil War in the old mining town of Weasua. There, the people lived in abject poverty despite unearthing the diamond wealth for nearly seven decades. Through that prism of poverty, disorganization, mismanagement, and resource abuse, I began to observe patterns and parallels between the town and the country's fragile state.

The town was settled by people avoiding the forced labor conscription to Fernando Po and the Firestone Rubber Plantation in the 1920s, similar to the origin of Liberia, which was settled by (freed) slaves fleeing the United States in the 1800s. Like the country's ruling class, who came from America and failed to develop Liberia, the town's early inhabitants neglected building Weasua from the riches they exploited from the ground.

A year later, when I returned to Monrovia, I encountered Alex Jones, my former classmate, who was also preoccupied with understanding the crises in the country.

Our discussions and analyses of the war encompassed the warlords, peacekeepers, political figures, and the peace agreements signed and violated by the warring factions. The subjects and activities of the interim governments, insurgencies, military, political, diplomatic, security, and economic maneuvers, as well as counter-strategies, would also be examined under the scope of our exercise.

Three decades later, I remained focused on Liberia as the themes, systems, and patterns I encountered began to form theories and ideas I could articulate. This led me to conclude that my findings were significant enough to justify writing a book. Most importantly, it had to be a book that echoes the aspirations of the people and aligns with the nation's destiny

Chapter 1:
The Case for Reform

The declaration for systematic, structural, and ideological changes and reforms in Liberia could not have come at a better time than now! When successive governments have pursued wrong policies and cannot deliver the people's basic needs. When presidents continue to expand the executive branch of government but beg foreign donors to fund those expenditures, and when the country is in the hands of one of the most corrupt, weakest, and most incompetent leadership ever. While the president masquerades as a knowledgeable and experienced politician, the legislature is plundering the country's coffers and further entrenching the state in chaos and mismanagement. A glaring example of that failure was the Executive and Judiciary branches' inability to hold the legislature accountable in 2024 for its actions. That negligence led to a crisis and culminated in the burning of the Capitol Building.

Amid these systemic political and economic crises, unemployment remains high, and the Liberian currency depreciates daily. The cost of living is unaffordable for millions of people, and ordinary civil servants' salaries are insufficient to cover living expenses; they are also often paid late, as in previous administrations.

The country's so-called sixty-one State-Owned Enterprises (SOEs) are disorganized and mismanaged under the Executive Branch of Government. While fifteen of these enterprises have failed, the remaining forty-six are underperforming and drained of their resources. These businesses cannot create jobs nor produce goods and services for the domestic market. Worse, the national budget pays the salaries and compensation of managers and executives at those mismanaged corporations. At the same time, presidents and high-ranking government officials funnel millions of dollars for themselves through payroll, corruption, bribes, and well-paying positions funded by foreign subsidies.

Every president, legislator, and top government official enters public office poverty-stricken but often leaves with significant wealth. Yet, how ordinary Liberian lives are improved, or employment is provided, or health and education are funded during these politicians' tenure, remains the billion-dollar unanswered question.

Just like presidents, legislators, and high-paid government officials who earn income above the cost of living, the solution to addressing poverty is to give money directly to individuals.

Money erases the suffering caused by poverty just as light dispels darkness. It is therefore vital to understand and acknowledge that money, as the primary solution for overcoming poverty, cannot be replaced by infrastructure development like roads, hospitals, electricity, and airports. If poverty is primarily measured by income, then the principal focus should be on making money accessible to individuals through various means. This approach would help them address the hardships caused by poverty, allowing them to pay for the services that these infrastructures provide and to enjoy the benefits they offer.

In developed countries, when an individual can't pay rent or buy food, they don't get new roads or electricity as a solution; instead, they get money or jobs. In Brazil, despite economic and political reforms and infrastructure development in the 2000s, both President Fernando Henrique Cardoso and President Luiz Inácio Lula da Silva introduced and expanded the 'Bolsa Família' cash transfer program. The direct cash payments to mothers (families) helped send children to school, relocate families from the slums, and lift millions out of poverty.

In America, a combination of disability payments, food stamps, charter schools, Section 8 vouchers, stimulus, and refunds is given to the poor to fight poverty. Even wealthy individuals, corporations, and businesses receive tax cuts, refunds, and rebates to address financial difficulties.

Shouldn't one conclude now that it is because of the income their presidents, legislators, and top government officials are earning that allows them and their families to live better lives, despite the poor infrastructure development? Therefore, don't be coerced into believing that electricity, school buildings, new hospitals, and good roads replace money as the answer to poverty.

Nyonblee Karnga-Lawrence, Darius Dillon, Edwin Snowe, Ellen Johnson Sirleaf, Abu Bana Kamara, Joseph Boakai, Mo Ali, and George Weah are thriving today, far beyond the reach of thousands of well-educated and skilled Liberian doctors, engineers, economists, and university professors, because of the income earned from the government. Income has become an equalizer among them. If that factor were removed, they would risk becoming beggars within a few months. So, why are Liberians being coerced into believing that roads and electricity solve the problem of poverty is beyond belief.

Liberian governments' standard operating protocol in managing the economy has also been begging foreign investors and donors for loans and grants to rebuild the country. Even though that method not only fails to work but also thwarts the country's growth and development, every president continues to make begging, charity, and foreign donations the key cornerstone of their political platform and economic plan.

Successive administrations are also inadvertently using outdated, rigid tax collection schemes to depress the economy, punish businesses, and exacerbate poverty. These charges leveled against legislators, presidents, and their administrations are evident in the bad fiscal policies they perpetuate and the country's economic mismanagement.

Many kids are out of school. They and their parents are stuck in poverty, with limited opportunities to build a better future. The number of children and adults selling a few pieces of merchandise, most of which are not worth more than five United States dollars, just to buy their daily meals, continues to increase. They roam the streets, their neighborhoods, and marketplaces daily under the hot sun and heavy rain, but still cannot find relief. Some fall into drug use, prostitution, and crimes. Others scavenge dump sites for plastic bags and aluminum cans to sell to buy food, which is scarce and expensive on the local market because Liberians primarily rely on food imports to feed themselves.

The men typically leave most agricultural and food production work to the women and children. After the men finish brushing, burning, and clearing small spots for farming, the women and children are left with the bulk of the tasks of planting the crops, scaring away the birds, and harvesting the rice. They are also responsible for drying and pounding the rice for consumption.

This division of labor demonstrates one of the main reasons the country's rice yield and food production are always low.

The Current Administration's National Agriculture Development Plan (NADP) 2024-2030, "Liberians Feed Yourselves Agenda" even echoed that same psychosis. The plan emphasizes the crucial role of women and youth in producing food for the nation, but says nothing about the roles and contributions of men in agriculture and food production.

Like previous administration attempts to invest in farming and food production, that plan methodologies and funding strategies are inadequate to outlive the administration. Therefore, such a plan is liable to be scrapped at the end of their tenure. Besides, if the Ministry of Agriculture presides over formulating the country's agricultural plan and food production, managing farms, and producing food, as that plan suggests, where are the independent regulatory structures and who enforces oversight?

There is also insufficient support for the blind, disabled, and deaf individuals from the Group of '77, which was established to assist people with disabilities. The organization is badly managed and many people with disabilities beg and live on the streets or get assistance from their families.

One of the reasons is that the office of the Vice President, which traditionally manages the organization and oversees staffing, spent most of the organization's funds on pay and compensation of the workers and staffed the organization with people who are predominantly of the Vice President's tribal group, their cycle of cronies and partisans.

Although the vice president's office is responsible for overseeing the organization's daily operations, funding for the Group has remained less than a million dollars each year for the past 18 years. In contrast, the vice president receives several million dollars annually to manage their own affairs within the same period.

Instead of allocating millions each year to the vice president's office to do nothing and head this organization, the position of vice president should be abolished! The millions from the vice president's office should be used as *Cash Transfers* disbursed to people with disabilities directly in the form of *Mobile Money* through their respective Districts.

In places like Waterside and many towns and villages across the country, countless young men and women wake up and go to bed under the same conditions. They face unchangeable circumstances daily.

Discussions with young people in places like Happy Corner, Down Waterside have revealed that this is the farthest some have traveled — or will ever travel — in search of better opportunities and improved living conditions.

Many young people across Africa are trapped in poverty and are often unsure about how their circumstances will improve. The elections of their favorite and most trusted politicians, who cannot improve their lives, worsen the problem, leaving them feeling more hopeless and frustrated than in previous elections.

The impending reforms will provide opportunities to maximize young people's vision, skills, talents, and energies through military service, employment, and entrepreneurship. Embedded within these reformed structures and frameworks will also be processes and strategies deployed to prevent the old, corrupt lawmakers, politicians, and former public officials from repeatedly using their tribes, political parties, and connections as revolving doors to public office and high paying positions. It also ensures that all elected offices are limited to two terms or a maximum of ten years in office.

At present, there are individuals in the country who seek and maintain elected positions perpetually. Their welfare takes priority, yet they provide no solutions or better policies in return for the higher living standards that the State and the People have given them. Although they pass bills to improve their own well-being and living conditions, it is impossible to identify a bill passed since the postwar era that benefits individual Liberians in similar ways.

The people are left to protect and fend for themselves. Right now, only a few people who live in Monrovia can afford to protect themselves and their homes. They mostly live in gated compounds with high fences and barbed wire to defend themselves against armed robbers and thieves. The rest of the people are expected to ensure their own security and safety, even though there is a government to whom they pay taxes to enforce the law and provide protection.

Monrovia is insecure and scary, especially at night. People are living in darkness, and the fear of the dark permeates everywhere. The incidents of drugs, crimes, and murders are overwhelming and unprosecuted; If caught, murderers, drug dealers, and criminals are imprisoned for a few months, after which they can either bribe their way out of jail or are released without facing further consequences.

Although police officers set up checkpoints everywhere (at night), they intimidate ordinary drivers and those earning a living more than they provide security and safety. The stature and physique of police officers are inferior. Besides being improperly selected, they are underpaid, poorly trained, inadequately equipped, and not properly uniformed.

In Congo Town, the police are stationed in an old, dilapidated, un-electrified building. When it is late at night, police officers cannot record their reports in the dark. Also, when civilians need police assistance, they must pay to transport police on motorcycles to attend to their cases or the scene of an accident.

Checkpoints along the main highways from various borders into the city are generally relaxed and manned by a few individuals. Most security personnel move their checkpoints far away from villages and towns. Worse, each unit - police, immigration officers, fire inspectors, and revenue officers (tax collectors) - seems to set up their own checkpoints at various points along the road or highway. In emergencies, they cannot help the residents, nor can the civilians come to their aid in case of an attack.

Along the country's dusty roads, some of the boys who hang out with the immigration and police officers at checkpoints in the interior at night take charge of the gates, while the officers are asleep, who should be inspecting the vehicles.

The same is not true when traveling at night in Ghana and Côte d'Ivoire. The security personnel on duty in those countries are always alert and attentive to their assignments. Their scrutiny of passengers is sometimes considered more rigid than necessary, but it keeps the people safe and their countries secure.

Liberia's ports of entry are also exposed, unprotected, and undefended to intrusion. The defense and security measures at the border are inferior to those of neighboring countries, and immigration protocols are even weaker in comparison.

Additionally, the country is particularly vulnerable and unguarded along the Atlantic Ocean, as there are no coast guards to patrol the shores, provide protection and deter criminals. It is impossible to know how the country is being exploited.

Witnesses at the Truth and Reconciliation Commission raised that issue and recommended that the country adopt a new mindset regarding defense, security, and law enforcement as its top priority. They advise that Liberia create a formidable, imposing, and capable national defense and security force that reflects the strength of a people and a nation that has experienced war and understands the need to take responsibility for their own security, safety, and well-being.

Such a powerful force could defend and safeguard the country, compelling neighboring countries to seriously consider the consequences of their actions before supporting any insurgency against Liberia again. Most importantly, they emphasized that the training and leadership structure of this new defense, security, and police force dedicated to the country comprises Liberian security experts, military strategists, and former warring generals, similar to those in Iraq and Afghanistan. Members of the Ba'ath Party and Taliban fighters reconstituted their countries' militaries.

But, the training and composition of the new Liberian Army disregarded those recommendations and the country's rich practical experiences and history of warmaking, combat, insurgencies, guerrilla tactics, and warfare maneuvers. They instead used foreign aid to rebuild the country's national defense and security, which probably didn't cover the cost of implementing such a strategy. They neglected to appoint capable wartime generals to lead the army, instead favoring those who were not associated with the war.

Those vulnerable defense and security lapses demonstrate that Liberians have probably not learned the lesson from the 1990 Rebel Incursion into the country. However, the election of Joseph Boakai, a long-time political crony and privileged politician, created the impression among Liberians that some of these key economic, security, safety, and defense issues would be addressed. Yet, Boakai (and his predecessors) have failed to establish effective security and defense strategies, to enforce robust legal safeguards, and to establish clear reforms, a better economic system, and vision for the country.

That is why this book, REFORM, is launching the first counteroffensive in that war against those practices, to bring about change and chart a new course for Liberia: to defend and protect the country, fight for genuine national ideals and plans, thrive economically, and exercise autonomy over its politics. Most importantly, the book is intended to reform the institutions of government, motivate the people, and educate a new brand of nation-builders to navigate the paths to sovereignty, national destiny, and improved living standards.

The book also seeks to dismantle the assault on Liberia's sovereignty and the external governance systems and practices imposed upon it.

This assault has persisted since the country's founding, serving as the primary driver of the civil war and its lasting hardships. Although it may not be apparent to the ordinary person, the destructive impact of these systems and structures has been so widespread and more devastating than the civil war and the guns and bullets that once littered the streets. They are also the root cause of the weak governments it has had, corruption, abuse of power, exploitation, and external control through financial and military means in the country.

This imposed governing system causes presidents, top government officials, judges, and lawmakers to become corrupt, to compensate themselves exorbitantly, behave in an unruly manner, and evade prosecution.

Such behavior is typical in countries where the three branches of the Republican form of government are practiced. Kenya, Liberia, Ghana, and Nigeria have some of the worst forms of those kinds of governments that many African nations are dealing with.

This is why foreign donors and corporations can also finance Liberia's elections, allowing citizens to vote while failing to achieve their desired outcomes. It is also why Liberians can elect presidents and lawmakers but cannot hold them accountable. This is why the president is the final arbiter of the country's economic and political systems and the administrator of justice, and no one can challenge it. This is why all the large corporations and financial concerns are foreign-owned.

In developed nations, their citizens own and operate their large corporations and hire foreigners to work for them. In Liberia and many African countries, their citizens work for foreigners. As a result, foreign individuals, nations, and their corporations gain considerable influence over an African country's politics, economy, growth, development, and infrastructure priorities. In these situations, countries often find that their defense, political, and economic objectives are gradually reshaped to align with the interests of these foreign corporations and their external donors who subsidize their national budgets.

As a Liberian reading this book, the question for you, this generation, and those to come is whether these long-standing ideas, practices, and systems will continue to dominate your lives and keep you at a disadvantage, or will the ideas and approaches in this book or those of your generation replace them?

Liberians have lived as people without introspection for a very long time now. Since independence, the country has been conditioned to think and behave more like Americans than Liberians. Although those who founded the nation came to this land as freed people, they nevertheless still thought and acted as if they were still **slaves**. Even though it has been nearly two centuries since the country's formation, that convoluted history, thought process, and behavior of a *slave* still haunt succeeding generations.

The first generation of leaders and settlers focused more on events in the U.S. than on building Liberia. They formed a government, social, and education system based on America. Students were conditioned to study American government, history, literature, and geography, but not Liberia's. The purpose of their education was to civilize and convert Indigenous Africans to Christianity, not nation-building. Subsequent generations continued that trend.

They taught their children to wear long tailcoats and top hats like their oppressors. To speak English well, but unable to think critically or demonstrate problem-solving skills.

Those who traveled to the United States for further studies pursued degrees in public administration, agriculture, the arts, and literature, but only returned home to serve in top government positions, like finance, public works, and telecommunications ministries and agencies, and hired foreigners to perform the technical work. While the Indigenous peoples were oppressed and forced to live as *subjects* and *domestic servants* of the ruling class. A few stripped of their African names and languages were acculturated into the attenuated *American Slave Culture* brought to these shores.

This was a prerequisite for assimilation, enabling one to integrate into society and benefit in their own country. Indigenous music, attire, and arts were banned in public. Their African traditions, cultures, and customs were ridiculed. Those in charge preferred everything American instead of Liberian.

Today, students know more about America's literature, history, and the Great Lakes, but nothing about Liberia's shadowy and poorly navigable rivers along the Atlantic Ocean. It is a problem that the new generation must solve!

They must think critically within and rectify those inequities. Fortunately, Indigenous music, arts, and literature are gradually emerging, but it is a concept that the new generation of Liberian artists, writers, reformers, advocates, and educators must continually stimulate!

The laws were enforced in a similar manner. High-ranking government officials and the ruling class were exempt from hut tax, and certain laws, but the Indigenous peoples suffered disproportionately from the grievous weight of those same laws. The ruling class, wealthy, and well-connected foreigners could ignore the law and justice system and violate the common man's rights and privileges without redress. Like the Israelites escaping slavery, they created special laws and privileges for themselves while forcing the original landowners into a system of discrimination and servitude.

Many of those exclusions and exceptionalism even became reserved in the power and authority of the presidency, from which the country is not far removed today. Such an ideology and attitude have made Liberians neither Americans nor Africans, but a misfit amongst Africans.

When the United States gained independence from Great Britain, it had to create a new identity and government to demonstrate its independence and sovereignty. The country had to focus on its own growth and work hard to become strong and competitive. Liberia, too, must break away, work hard, and establish its own unique identity, a view of itself and the world.

When Guinea became independent from France, it had an adversarial relationship with its former colonizer after France vandalized its capital. That behavior dictated how Guineans dealt with France.

After Liberia's independence, France and Britain continued to encroach upon Liberia's territory from their colonial positions. Although Liberia complained to America, their interventions did nothing to return Liberia's lands. Yet, Liberia did not invade those territories nor deal with France and Britain as adversaries. Because Liberia failed to do so, the dependency mentality of always relying on others to solve its problems still lingers.

It undermines the fundamental understanding of Liberians' responsibility for themselves versus the assistance they may seek from others. Perhaps this is one reason why the country's sovereignty is disregarded when deciding what is in its best interest, why Liberia's economic and political problems and social upheavals are often worse in size and scope, and why the people struggle to solve their problems as solutions seem imported from America rather than developed from within.

A similar attitude has led Liberia to be viewed as more feminine compared to Guinea, Côte d'Ivoire, and Sierra Leone. While most people around the world refer to their countries as their "Father's Land," such as Russia, Germany, the United States, Ghana, China, and Nigeria, Liberians call their country "Mama Liberia."

This mindset influences attitudes, national identity, and other societal aspects, as seen in Liberia.

The psychology of a person coming from their "Father's House" is entirely different from that of their "Mother's." It also affects how such a person perceives and interacts with the world. As a result, while men in West Africa seem to be leading their countries, women in Liberia appear to be in charge-holding positions such as the presidency, vice presidency, Chief of Staff, Minister of Defense, Chief Justice, and the Senate Pro Tempore.

Liberia is also consistently seeking and lobbying for external assistance. Since gaining independence, Guinea has built and maintained a strong military and does not depend on other countries for defense and protection. But Liberia's experience has been different.

In 1979, during the Rice Riot, the country had to call on Guinea for help to quell its protests. On occasions, even Sierra Leone had to rely on the Guinean military for support.

Sierra Leone, Guinea, and Côte d'Ivoire have also used the weaknesses at Liberia's borders to support incursions into the country without retaliation.

When Côte d'Ivoire supported the war from Liberia's northern border in 1990, the country didn't launch a counterattack or invade parts of Côte d'Ivoire's territory. It had to rely on neighboring countries for support and peacekeeping efforts instead. Despite these histories of military aggression, the country has not significantly developed or expanded its military over the last thirty years. It has always had a small, weak army, a fragile government, and ineffective law enforcement practices, constantly seeking "outside help."

Since 1912, the United States has trained and equipped the Liberian Armed Forces, but the country's defense and protection remain ineffective.

The country ranks 15th out of 16 nations in West Africa in terms of military strength, making it one of the weakest and unable to defend itself or pose any significant threat. More than thirty years have passed since the war, and despite the training and funding it has received, the Liberian Army still lacks essential equipment such as planes, helicopters, gunboats, and radar detection systems along its coast.

For instance, Retired General Charles Julu, who led the Armed Forces of Liberia (AFL) as a Frontline Commander during the first few months of the 1990 Civil War, testified at the Truth and Reconciliation Commission Hearing that the government had only about 300 men fighting against the insurgency. Could exploring alternative ways of recruiting, training, and equipping the army and security forces change that trajectory?

The country is also led by a group of men who do not establish large farms or build massive infrastructure projects to demonstrate the *"Strength and Power of their Masculinity"*.

Countries that construct massive infrastructure projects independent of other foreign nations exhibit those masculine traits and power. Such a trait is visible in any nation led by self-reliant, sovereign, and self-governing men. Liberia has instead depended on other countries, their donor organizations, and corporations to construct small roads, public buildings, and various public works projects in the country. Therefore, it can be argued that Liberia's large buildings and major infrastructure have been built by foreigners rather than by Liberians.

Amidst these schemes, the government cannot generate revenue (taxes) to fund and coordinate public administration and services. As a result, millions are jobless; there are millions more who are going hungry, malnourished, and homeless daily.

The country's education system is ruined, underfunded, and devalued. Priority is not given to funding higher education and skill development locally.

Students graduate from high schools and universities without being able to think critically and demonstrate the necessary skills to compete in the job market or contribute to nation-building. Therefore, a new concept of education, critical thinking, and nation-building must be developed to replace the current system.

It should not be one that solely relies on foreign universities and nations for advancements and research but one where advancements are homegrown and nurtured, where tuition is paid per child to attend their school of choice, where college graduates can spend time in the villages and towns and write about them, where people can learn, research and develop solutions to their problems in their respective districts.

Under such an arrangement, the government can no longer export solutions from Monrovia nor own and manage learning institutions, hire teachers, and manage supplies and overhead. Instead, the proprietors of those institutions will manage and administer schools.

Districts will be required to innovate and develop local solutions to address their own problems. The government's role and responsibility will be to regulate schools, learning, and funding.

Public healthcare services will also undergo similar reforms. A more effective and alternative healthcare sector will require significant investments and an insurance scheme that covers individuals, which differs from what currently exists.

As the government steps back from running hospitals and clinics, hiring medical staff, and managing funds, Liberians in the private sector will have the opportunity to take charge. The government's role and responsibility will be to provide funding, establish regulations, and enforcement.

More businesses, expertise, and institutions will be established to support and regulate the healthcare sector, create jobs, and provide essential goods and services.

The country is presently dealing with unaffordable Basic Medical Care Services, primarily managed by private providers, foreign donors and non-profit organizations. Public officials, presidents, and lawmakers travel abroad for better medical treatment, while ordinary citizens are left behind to struggle with a dysfunctional healthcare system they cannot afford.

As the country gets trapped in this vicious cycle of high illiteracy rate, unhealthy populace, unemployment, low living standards, inefficiencies, and corruption, foreign vulture finance combines are in the background peddling "structural adjustment programs," proposing more cuts to civil servants' salaries and public services, championing lower living standards, and dismantling the last safety net of an already struggling people and nation. Yet, the roles of these foreign financiers are shielded from untrained eyes.

Their objective here is to keep countries like Liberia perpetually in debt, weak, and compromised as much as possible, while silently stripping them of any agency to solve their problems or defend themselves.

A clear example of this was the Millennium Challenge Corporation's $270 million funding in Liberia. In the mid-2000s, the organization identified roads and electricity as the primary obstacles to Liberia's economic growth and development, rather than the absence of banks and large corporations.

The Ellen Johnson Sirleaf Administration at the time agreed. The funds provided the country with a small hydro dam and a few paved roads, but the power supply remains unreliable and inadequate to meet the needs of homes, factories, and businesses. Moreover, the economic condition is worse.

This example illustrates how an outsider's institution can influence and shape a country's growth, development, and investment goals and objectives, especially in the absence of national economic, defense and development plans.

Second, that project was awarded not because it addressed the country's short and long-term electrical problems or was investment-worthy, but because it satisfied the threshold for aid, loans, and grants.

If Liberia had directed that fund into creating banks, the money supply would have increased, allowing for the creation of corporations, factories, and jobs.

Although that project might have provided electric current to a few thousand homes, most of their customers are still unemployed and cannot afford the bills. Most people still have to rely on solar panels and backup generators to power their homes, businesses, factories, and facilities. But the government and the project's funder(s) continue to champion the hydro as a worthwhile project that also attracts investments.

On the contrary, from the 1940s through the 1970s, Liberian Governments did not have to build roads or provide electricity to attract investors like Firestone, Liberia Mining Company (LMC), and Liberian American Swedish Mining Company (LAMCO). Those companies came in and constructed their roads and powered their corporations. So, why didn't Ellen Johnson's government adopt a similar approach?

The two examples, donor funding and private investment, show the country's incoherent growth, development, and investment strategies. Foreign donors and private investors fund projects and investments where they get the most rewards, not merely because of the countries' interests.

The third proposition is the country's own outlook on growth, not what they are offered.

So, where is Liberia's own approach to growth, development, and investment in the mix of such trade-offs and swaps? The examples show that there isn't any to follow.

National Plan

In the 1999 Central Bank Act, Charles Taylor's Government amended the National Bank Act to make the Central Bank responsible for growth and development, not foreign donors and funders.

Unfortunately, succeeding presidents and their administrations, lawmakers, and central bank governors have not followed that law. They are probably unaware of that provision within the Central Bank Act, or are unaware of the mechanics of the law.

The new approach to growth, development, and investment should be outlined in a *National Plan* that clearly expresses the country's goals and objectives. A provision of the law stipulated above should be included in the *National Plan* so that everyone knows which agency is responsible for growth(employment), development, and investment, not the president.

Instead of a president flaunting development and growth targets or the backers of aid, loans, and various types of external development and investments entering the country, dictating their own machinations, and suggesting a development plan, they must be subjected to an already established National Plan.

A plan not based on the platform of the candidates vying for office or the political party in power. But one that no single individual, president, or external interest can create, control, or alter. It should be established by the people and modified when they see fit. And neither by any foreign entity, because backers of external assistance, such as loans, foreign direct investments, and technical assistance, are notorious for coming in with their plans, keeping third-world nations chronically indebted and compromised, and not generating a return on investment.

Furthermore, the plan must be free of so-called *"foreign experts' or consultants' advice,"* often skewed in favor of these donors, lenders, and investment underwriters, rather than the recipient countries.

Another reason why Liberia's approaches to growth, development, investment, education, healthcare, and other key areas vary widely depending on the president is that the country lacks a fixed National Plan that successive administrations must follow. Those in power dictate the country's growth, development, and investment plans, instead of following an established path.

This way of thinking and behaving can be directly attributed to American governing theory. In the United States, foreign policies, tax schemes, and economic platforms swing like a pendulum every four or eight years, depending on which political party wins the election. Those policies are further tailored to align with the incumbent president's preferences and directives. This is precisely what

Liberia has replicated. But as a small country, these swift and sudden policy changes have serious and costly consequences.

Instead, Liberia should create a long-term national plan spanning 3, 5, 10, or 25 years, covering growth, development, investment, taxation, public finance, employment, education, healthcare, prosecuting crimes, and other relevant areas. Future governments would be required to follow this plan, just like in countries such as Singapore and China. It will work well for Liberia and save the country from costly turnovers and unfinished ventures.

This National Plan should specify the percentages of mandatory and discretionary spending that should be allocated to defense and law enforcement, education, growth and development, healthcare, investments, districts, cash transfers, home construction, and other relevant areas in the National Budget.

In that system, the Central Bank will disburse payments and enforce these measures. With such an arrangement, a legislature will not need to pass a budget, and a president will not need to sign it into law. But the recipient ministries and agencies will have the latitude to distribute the funds internally as they see fit.

The plan must include the proposed design and layout of all the country's highways, train tracks, and airports. It must also demonstrate the country's plan for electrification and internet infrastructure, its ability to feed itself, and its potential for agricultural development. The plan must also stipulate the percentage of the minerals that would be mined and apportioned for the National Gold, Diamond, and Mineral Reserves versus those exported.

The National Plan and spending metrics should be evaluated quarterly and reviewed annually by the advisory council, not the president, and the people can amend the plan every 3, 5, 7, and 10 years.

Under the Revenue Code - Title 36, for instance, only the president determines and approves the quantities of gold the country exports. But it is the foreign corporations and illegal miners, not the State-Owned Enterprises, that are mining, producing, controlling, and exporting gold and minerals out of the country. The remaining portion is smuggled across borders into neighboring countries.

If foreign corporations are mining, producing, and exporting gold, how can the president decide how much gold to keep or export when they are not in charge of gold production? That failure of the country to establish a National Gold or Minerals Reserve is directly attributed to the president's failure, but no one can challenge the president.

There are no plans to lay out what should be done with the rent received from the oil blocks auctioned to foreign corporations. Neither are there plans that outline how many national corporations should be created to provide jobs for Liberians, nor which branch of government should establish them. Although there are laws governing how corporations should register and operate, decisions regarding national planning, investment, growth, and development are left entirely to the president.

No matter how inexperienced or incompetent these individuals may be or how bad their ideas are, Liberian presidents have always had the final say, and no one has been able to change that. Despite their plans being discarded at the end of their term in office and the new presidents adopting a new and different plan from their predecessors, costing the country millions in growth, lost development, and investments, no one seems to identify this as a problem. But this book has, and it proposes that it should be fixed through the National Plan.

For example, the old Ministry of Defense building was partially constructed under Samuel Doe's Administration in the 1980s but was destroyed and replaced with the new Ministerial Complex under Ellen Johnson Sirleaf in the 2000s.

The only system in place to plan and evaluate such a decision before the president takes action is the National Planning Council, which the president unilaterally controls.

According to Title 12 of the Liberian Code of Laws Revised, the Council is chaired by the President of Liberia and includes all cabinet ministers as members. Additionally, the Council comprises the Director General of the General Services Agency, the Director General of Action for Development and Progress, and the Director of the Budget. The Minister of Planning and Economic Affairs serves as the Executive Secretary of the Council. The president also appoints other persons as members of the National Planning Council and invites other Government officials or private citizens to attend its meetings occasionally.

In this example, the president has exclusive control over national planning and development. Based on such an arrangement, what prevents the current president from steering the country in the wrong direction or future presidents from discarding the predecessors' plan if a better system is not implemented to address such a problem, especially when the outgoing president's plan was better for the country?

As part of the proposed National Plan, this book recommends that, in the future, the Advisory Council, not the president, should evaluate, appraise, steer, and preside over the national plan, investments, growth, and development plans, and decide the country's course of action. And these councils will operate independently of the president, and the president cannot be a part of the council.

The fundamental contours of that National Plan must first address the purpose of the State, national language, faith, define the structures of government, and the management of resources. It should also address the country's defense, protection, and competitive advantages. This is followed by the individual's place in society - their value, hopes, aspirations, and benefits from the State, and what they should also expect to contribute to the State in return.

This plan will be like the nation's technical manual, written in clear and concise language that is easy to read and understand.

Next, everyone, not just the president and government officials, should be taught and become aware of the core features of the National Plan, including its benefits, responsibilities, and consequences.

The summary of this plan should be printed on a poster and posted in public places, such as offices, schools, churches, and ports of entry, so that everyone is aware of and understands the country's direction. It should be taught to students, public servants, and especially those seeking public office.

This ensures that no one will assume public office, work in government, or do business with the State and profess ignorance of their requirements and expectations. When the State is not being managed properly, people will know where the problem originates, who or what is at fault, and how to solve it.

This way, when someone is placed in charge of certain offices and is responsible for executing specific tasks but fails, they will be aware of the consequences.

For instance, if a president attempts to change the constitution to extend their term in office or alter the election result, the plan will stipulate the crimes committed, the consequences for all those involved, and the administration's overthrow.

The plan must also stipulate the punishment of civil servants engaging in bribes and corruption; when the accused is arrested, their bail should be equivalent to the amount they are charged with stealing before they are released. Their bank accounts should be seized, and their properties should be sold to pay restitution if they are found guilty. The consequence of such a law will also affect individuals and institutions that do business or receive money from the government.

Following such education and awareness, presidents and leaders cannot claim innocence regarding the National Plan or its consequences when they violate the law.

During elections, no candidate, whether for president, county management or mayor, shall be allowed to create their own economic, defense, healthcare, education, or foreign policy plans. Instead, they will be restricted to the national plan. Political debates and campaigns will focus on how well each candidate can support and improve the National Plan. That is one proposition Liberians have not tried yet.

They have rewritten the constitution, overthrown governments, fought wars, tried dictatorial rule, and elected experienced politicians in pursuit of change. But the results they seek appear to be more elusive than ever.

Over the last 18 years, new presidents have been elected, and political parties have come to office and left, recycling different frivolous policies by successive administrations. Politicians, lawmakers and presidents' lives have improved, but the circumstances and living conditions of millions of Liberians have either remained the same or worsened, and change is nowhere to be found. Today, Liberians are no closer to a solution than 45 years ago.

Suppose a National Plan or an approach of greater magnitude is not thoughtfully considered and implemented? In that case, the country is liable to continue meandering through the hands of more incompetent administrations, economic mismanagement, and political instabilities and insecurities.

The initial approach to adopting such a National Plan is to first hold a referendum on this manifesto or a similar plan to bring about this change, rather than immediately undertaking constitutional reform, as countries have often done. Because the Constitution is designed to serve as a principle for governance and guidelines for directives, policy-making, and execution, it does not plan a country.

This up-and-down vote on such a referendum will establish whether the country wants to go in a different direction or remain on course. Votes on subsequent referendums will follow the first referendum until all the fundamental reforms and restructuring are established and implemented, after which a Constitution Reform can be held.

In conclusion, fellow citizens, the journey to national rebirth, liberty, and independence is never attained without blood, sweat, and tears. But this declaration of national renewal and devotion will require much more of Liberians' patriotism, sacrifices, resolve, creativity, and tenacity.

Yes, Liberians have fought wars, torn the country apart, and even overthrown presidents in the hope of building a better nation in pursuit of true independence. But *Real Change*, a *True National Rebirth*, will only happen when the people have a single focus and directive through a National Plan that everyone is held to. No matter how Liberians prioritize their love for the country over personal gain and short-term benefits, only a plan for the country will direct the fortresses of their minds, shape their ideas and aspirations, and collectively strengthen their will to do the right thing in the same direction and give the country their best.

This endeavor must confront and withstand both the visible and invisible forces present and those that lie ahead. So, whenever any Liberian must choose between country, individual, and external interests and threats, they can muster the agency to select what is best for Liberia first, before any other, regardless of the circumstances.

Poor nations with national plans and a clear focus on pursuing their goals and objectives, aiming for a better future, are often demeaned, ridiculed, and undermined at the beginning.

Remember the emergence of China's manufacturing might in the 1970s and 80s? Every product from China that came to Liberia was considered inferior. People preferred Western-made goods. Today, not only Liberia but the world depends on Chinese products.

The ideas and strategies in this book won't only transform Liberia, but can become the spark for remaking the rest of Africa. Therefore, at some point in time, Liberians will be condemned to the same fate through propaganda, sabotage and aggression, whether knowingly or unknowingly, and treated like people in Cuba, Haiti, Burkina Faso, Rwanda, Mali, and Niger who have undertaken similar tasks of bettering themselves.

Those countries are still reeling from the exploits of neocolonialism, sabotage, oppression, exploitation, and foreign control - external powers that are still attempting to usurp their sovereignties. Until Liberians become like people in Singapore who succeeded in remaking themselves and forging a better country and future for themselves and posterity, no one will treat Liberians with respect and dignity. If not, the country will continue to possess abundant material wealth, but will live as beggars when they fail.

Singapore is an example of one of those countries with a population comparable to Liberia, but it has built a strong, successful, and resilient nation based on a sound National Plan. They resolved to improve their lives and fortunes out of nothing. But most importantly, they did not flinch in the face of adversaries and aggressors.

Liberians can follow Singapore's example, establish ambitious goals, and accomplish remarkable things if they remain committed to a solid National Plan with clear objectives. Until the country unites around that shared vision and destiny and successfully unravels the misconceptions, practices, structures, and systems perpetuating poverty, subjugation, exploitation, and dependency, and becomes a nation that aspires to its values and destiny, it will remain a defeated, poor and struggling nation unable to help itself and find its place in the world.

Chapter 2:
The Purpose of The State

Liberia can be compared to Haiti and Somalia as examples of States pursuing wrong purposes or lacking a clear purpose. Symptoms of a country with misguided purposes or absence of purpose include internal conflict, economic stagnation, lawlessness, and political instability, all of which are present in the countries named above.

On the contrary, Rwanda's, Ghana's, and Mauritius' purposes are quite definitive and striking. They are reflected in the security and defense of their people, the rule of law and enforcement, their attitude, living standard, peace, and tranquility within their respective borders.

To reformulate Liberia's purpose, the people first need to engage in dialogues and debates and explicitly redefine the country's purpose regarding its goals and aspirations. These debates should be exhaustive, take place in every district, and develop into petitions endorsed through referendums.

The objectives of these discussions should be to outline the people's views and plans, along with the steps to achieve them, in unambiguous terms. For instance, if Liberia is considering configuring a strong defense, security, and law enforcement infrastructure, the referendum must discuss how Liberia plans to protect and defend itself, at what cost, and what measures it will take to provide security. How does the country plan to finance the government, development, and standard of living? What are or should be the country's competitive advantages compared to others? What makes one a Liberian?

The results of these deliberations must be comprehensive, organized and calibrated to reflect the psyche, purpose and functions of a new country, including the new roles and responsibilities of citizenship. They should outline new roles and responsibilities for the government, specifying how policies will be implemented and resources will be managed. They should also establish clear conduct and expectations for public officials, both in and out of office. A clear mission statement must be created to define Liberia's purpose, identity, vision, and worldview. This statement will serve as the country's brand and form a portion of the proposed National Plan.

Purpose is a common trait that countries share, regardless of their population, size, and natural resources, which determines their rankings among other nations worldwide. It also helps explain why a country and its citizens display certain intrinsic characteristics and behaviors.

For instance, Russia, North Korea, and Germany are considered tough masculine nations. Nations that are considered masculine are often militarily strong and formidable. It is, therefore, through such specter that the world has viewed and related to them.

In West Africa, Guinea is regarded as a strong and masculine nation. The country boasts a robust and formidable military. Its peacekeeping forces were exceptionally disciplined and proved significantly more effective among other troops during the Economic Community of West African States Monitoring Group (ECOMOG) peace mission in Liberia.

Furthermore, for many Liberians, if someone declares that they are a Ghanaian or an American, a certain image or perception comes to mind.

Ghanaian citizenship evokes an image of someone who loves their country above all else. For whatever reason, Ghanaians believe that their country is the "*best.*" Many Ghanaian claim that every Black, successful, and accomplished person born in the West has their ancestry tied to Ghana. Regardless of how *trivial* it may seem, that ideology has helped Ghana project a certain image and philosophy, and has influenced the people to live and carry themselves in a particular way.

So, the idea that Ghana has become the home or primary destination for Black Americans repatriating to Africa today should be no surprise because their thinking has contributed to that way of life.

People around the world tend to also relate to Americans similarly. American citizenship, for instance, projects an image of a group of people living well and enjoying the excesses of material wealth.

Second, it conveys the notion of a people protected by their government and afforded considerable freedom and liberty, which is not typical worldwide. Even among Americans within the United States, citizenship is essentially the same in principle.

The citizenship of an Arab, Mexican, White, Black, or Chinese American is as good as that of a German or British American. This characteristic of America reflects another purpose of the United States.

So, if someone identifies as Liberian, what comes to mind? What does it mean? What does the name Liberia even signify as a State to you as a citizen?

About 60 years ago, China, India, and Brazil were poor, less productive, and uncompetitive nations. After finding their purpose as world-class leaders in their own right, they began to produce abundant goods and services and raise living standards among their people.

Today, the world recognizes them as leading economies globally. Chinese, Indian, and Brazilian citizenship also portray a different role and image today than they did half a century ago.

Second, Britain's purpose as an empire remains unchanged, even after its fall. Although the country is about the size of Ghana and has fewer natural resources in comparison, it sees itself and behaves as its leader. Even within the Commonwealth, where Britain is smaller and less populated than Canada, India and Nigeria, it still acts as their leader. This mindset is also why Britain struggled to be just a member in the European Union rather than being in charge.

Like Britain, the United States, one of its former colonies, refused to be a part of any organization just as a member instead of its head because it displayed similar thinking and disposition.

The United States also vowed never to be dominated by any foreign power, not even Britain. Yet, many former colonized countries remain hooked under France's and Britain's rule and do not see the concept of their *independence* and relationship as *adversarial* to their former European colonists.

That second example illustrates the similarities and use of purpose between the United States and Britain. Relations between Burkina Faso, Mali, Niger and France within the last few years are exactly how former colonized people have to deal with and interact with European nations until relations are reset on a mutual basis.

Purpose has different and far-reaching effects in countries like South Sudan and Eritrea, which were created and bonded together to protect themselves against aggressors.

Take Eritrea, which has had to defend itself against Ethiopia. One result of that type of purpose was the creation of a large and formidable military. Despite being a small country with a population similar to that of Ogun State in Nigeria, Eritrea has a military strength that is roughly half the size of Nigeria's estimated 230,000-strong military force, according to Global Fire Power. Interestingly, the Eritrean Army consists of 90,000 personnel, which exceeds Nigeria's army of 65,000, as reported by the same source. It was only through defining and cultivating its purpose that Eritrea could achieve such a defense posture.

Others, like Singapore and Cuba, were created for economic reasons but took different paths when they observed that their countries were being exploited.

Since 1959, Cuba, a country smaller and less endowed with mineral resources than Liberia, has fought against neo-colonialism and all forms of control to stay independent. Its constitution clearly states that Cuba opposes economic exploitation, oppression, and colonial rule. It still fights for those causes today. They even helped many African countries liberate themselves from the system of European colonial bondage.

Despite all the sanctions, external threats, and aggressions, Cuba's purpose has stood the test of time. They have remained resolved, united, and resilient in that cause. Furthermore, they protect and defend their citizens and provide them with better education and healthcare services.

The people in Bolivia displayed a similar sense of purpose when they protested against their government and a foreign corporation that monopolized their drinking water. Even though Bolivia's Constitution promises that everyone has the right to water, the government made a deal with Bechtel Corporation, a foreign company, to take control of the country's water supply.

Feeling betrayed and disenfranchised, the people rose in rebellion. In the end, the deal was canceled. The administration retreated, and Bechtel was expelled from the country.

Many former colonized nations and people have also changed their constitutions, names, and purposes if or when the purpose they inherited from their colonizers does not work for them, as we see in the countries above, including Mali, Niger, Burkina Faso and Rwanda.

Burkina Faso was formerly known as Upper Volta under French rule. But they changed their name to Burkina Faso - the Land of Upright Men - to reflect their purpose, view, and philosophy of a new and different country in the 1980s. After an intermittent period of interference by their former colonizer, aided by another visionless leader, the country has returned to its purpose under a new, young, and vibrant leader. Within a brief period, the new leader has raised living standards and spurred a vision of purpose and a freed people resisting foreign exploitation.

In Rwanda, we see a people who have not only changed their country and remained to live as a proud people since 1994, according to their new constitution, but are also "committed to preventing and punishing the crime of genocide and its ideology in all its manifestations."

Their history shapes their way of life and shows how they interact with the world. But many former colonies today struggle to understand their purpose or even question if they have one.

As more nations focus on or reflect on their purposes and use them to measure success or failure, their purpose will either become a key to new opportunities or a chain that keeps them trapped. Furthermore, the strangled France, Belgium, Britain, and other European nations holding over them will either crumble or become entrenched. And for people in Congo, Haiti, Somalia, and Liberia who remain dedicated to the proposition of statehood but lack that intangible virtue of purpose, they will exist but not thrive.

It does not matter whether it is between North and South Korea, Nigeria, or Norway. Purpose appears to tread as that common fate they all share. It determines if a state fails or succeeds, including the rise and fall of great states and empires.

When Liberia "served as the homeland for free blacks returning from the United States." It was a sanctuary for Black people worldwide seeking peace and freedom. It welcomed Black Americans fleeing the United States after the American Civil War through the 1970s and served as a home for African revolutionaries fighting for liberation across the continent.

During the 1986 Constitutional Reform, the Military Ruling Junta changed Liberia's purpose "to the pursuit of national unity, from a land established for black people seeking freedom."

Unfortunately, the country today does not serve as *"the sanctuary"* for Black People seeking freedom and liberty from around the world, nor does the image, lifestyle, and behavior of its citizens reflect a *"united people."* The country's outlook suggests that national unity is a vague concept, and proof of that is the absence of *"national unity"* everywhere.

Liberians are not safe, and secure either. The country is experiencing lawlessness, dysfunctional resource management, and increased corruption. People in one part of the country appear apathetic to the problems their fellow citizens face in other parts. Public leaders are corrupt, unethical, and self-serving. It is difficult to find their common causes or a common national language Liberian speak.

The Civil War clearly showed this deep division, with Americo-Liberians, Indigenous tribes, and the government all fighting against each other. Many people believed the war was only targeting *President Samuel Doe, his ethnic group, and his supporters*. Other tribes and counties failed to join the ruling administration's fight against *Charles Taylor*. But the war ended up victimizing everyone.

Furthermore, every ruling administration appears to be the most disuniting, oppressive, and challenging problem among the people. Those in government do not conduct themselves with a sense of patriotism, accountability, and purpose in their undertakings.

For example, presidents and lawmakers pay themselves disproportionately higher than other public employees. Presidential appointments are highly favored along partisan, family, and tribal lines, and the law favors those in government and their benefactors who can purchase justice. This outlook portrays a people and a country that are living with the wrong purpose. Therefore, Liberians need to redefine their "purpose" that aligns with their current and future realities.

In South Africa, as in Liberia, we see a group of people struggling to find or live within their purpose. After ending apartheid, they settled for "A Rainbow Nation," only to self-impose economic exclusion and disenfranchisement upon themselves. Black South Africans are aware of their predicament and constraints in bringing about change because they are pursuing the wrong purpose.

Many Black South Africans still do not own land and live in impoverished communities. Their economic mobility looks bleak for the foreseeable future. Unless the majority of Black South Africans control the country's economic and financial wealth, and their Central Bank is willing to intervene to significantly improve its citizens' living standards, "land appropriation without compensation" will remain an illusion.

Unlike South Africa, Singapore, a small island lacking mineral resources, has pursued unconventional means to develop and improve its people's living standards. Their commitment to staying independent from any nation or group has remained unshaken. It is also among some of the best-managed countries and economies in the world. Although once a British colony, Singapore successfully fended off Britain's attempts to manipulate and exert control over its sovereign wealth fund.

America also resisted Britain in 1775 when it taxed and denied them representation. America revolted against Britain's colonial rule and declared independence. After defeating Britain, they pledged to wage war on Britain, friends and foes, and anyone who attempted to impede upon their freedom, liberty, and pursuit of happiness.

Since then, America has remained on the offensive against advances to recolonization and exploitation. This is also one reason why no foreign media, religion, banks, commerce, or external interests can dominate any sphere within the United States' economic, political, and social life, particularly not Britain. That is why the American ruling class finds *TikTok's* dominance in its media space unacceptable.

Unfortunately, developing nations have not taken such an adversarial stance against former colonial powers. For example, over 40 African countries, including Liberia print their money in Britain, France, and Germany. Countries like Ghana, Sierra Leone, and South Africa even relied on British central bankers for financial advice and guidance.

In what capacity does Britain offer these countries its *"financial expertise"*? Does she do so as a partner, an empire, or a former colonizer, especially when these countries' economies continue to suffer worse financial and economic problems during and after Britain's presence?

Moreover, Britain was not involved in Liberia's peace process or post-war recovery efforts. Yet, its overt economic operations can be viewed based on several results:

InfraCo Africa, Hamak Gold Limited, British International Investment, Equatorial Palm Oil are just a few of the British companies currently dominating Liberia's economy. Second. Liberia's exiled President, Charles Taylor, is serving a life prison sentence in Britain.

What has Britain done or offered in exchange for such economic rewards? Do Britain's interests and purpose remain unchanged even in a small country like Liberia?

As shown above, nations' purposes and motives vary but continue to determine how countries function in relation to one another, whether for good or bad.

International organizations, such as the World Bank and the International Monetary Fund, apply similar ideologies and behaviors when dealing with underdeveloped nations.

Liberians need to rethink their purpose and act accordingly. They must decide what to support, protect, oppose, or prevent for their own good-including fighting harmful habits-to demand the change they want and in order to gain respect.

Nations without a clear purpose or those pursuing the wrong ones can harm themselves and even others. Liberia's pursuit of *"Unity"* as its primary purpose or goal, instead of robust sovereignty, law and order, and economic growth and development, is an example of a wrong pursuit.

As a result, crucial aspects of managing a functioning state, such as sovereignty, accountability, proper stewardship, law enforcement, and order, are being swapped in exchange for constructing roads, government buildings, farms and providing electricity. That is accompanied by an inferiority complex that permits them to subject their economic, political, social, defense, and management of the State to other nations, organizations, and corporations. It is also evident in the people's disorganization, bewilderment, and unruliness.

That recipe has produced a succession of corrupt and incompetent leaders and governments, extreme poverty, and increased the interference of capital finance and foreign interests. In the country's search for solutions, the people went to war, leading to the destruction of the country, the deaths of hundreds of thousands of people, the murder of two presidents, and the exile of another. Yet, the solutions appeared more elusive.

Furthermore, Liberia has allowed other nations and institutions to manage its economy, elections, and take over its military in the hopes of improvement, but this has not materialized.

Liberians have also adopted unfiltered Western governing theories, ideologies, and systems. Unfortunately, they are antithetical to caring for the community - *Liberia's way of life, values, and culture.* In areas where these systems are implemented without significant changes, a majority of the people are alienated, their lives disrupted by poverty, and they are forced to live in slums. These systems instead benefit the ruling elites, including the president, lawmakers, wealthy and well-connected individuals, and large businesses.

For example, over the past 18 years, successive regimes have implemented economic and financial policies and programs dictated by the United Nations, the World Bank, the African Development Bank, and the International Monetary Fund (IMF) rather than their own. Yet, living conditions have continued to decline.

These programs and policies are accompanied and reinforced by formally trained bureaucrats from global institutions like the World Bank and the

International Monetary Fund. These bureaucrats are frequently recycled in and out of developing nations' governments to orchestrate the World Bank and the International Monetary Fund schemes. When the mission is complete, they return to their institutions or employers.

While Western governments are less likely to hire bureaucrats with such credentials in top finance and central banking positions, African countries appear to be unaware of their infatuation with or insatiable cravings for hiring individuals with such resumes.

These profiles are quite common among African finance ministers and central bank managers like Mamo Mihretu, Governor of the National Bank of Ethiopia (NBE), and Dr. Kamau Thugge, Governor of the Central Bank of Kenya (CBK), respectively. In Nigeria, Ngozi Okonjo-Iweala, the Director General of the World Trade Organization, also played a similar role and function for her foreign employer (World Bank) as finance minister in her country's government.

In Liberia, almost all of the country's finance ministers in the last 18 years, from Antoinette Sayeh to Augustine Ngafuan(current and two-time finance minister), including Ellen Johnson Sirleaf, fit this profile, and the unhealthy state of Liberia's economy reflects that.

A relevant example is Amara Konneh, a former finance minister of Liberia. After serving in his country's government, he was hired by the World Bank and later returned to government.

While heading Liberia's financial sector, he received prestigious recognition in the foreign press. However, despite the accolades he received from abroad, his performance ultimately harmed the national economy.

Those who promoted him failed to communicate two critical points: First, the economy he managed was heavily reliant on charitable contributions, foreign donations, and rent. As a result, he did not need to demonstrate exceptional financial acumen or implement effective growth policies to grow the economy.

Second, he aligned public policies with the interests of his future employer, effectively exchanging these policies for draconian loans and debt relief. This left Liberia burdened with significant financial obligations and detrimental economic arrangements.

During his tenure as Finance Minister, Amara Konneh received hundreds of millions of dollars in aid, grants, and loans to combat Ebola. However, he left office without instituting measures or establishing a single factory to produce essential items such as gloves, chlorine, face masks, or protective gowns. As a result, when COVID-19 struck in 2020, the country scrambled for these vital supplies again.

After serving as finance minister, the World Bank Group hired Konneh to lead the Global Hub for Fragility, Conflict, Violence, and Forced Displacement (FCV). In 2024, he returned to public service by being elected as a Senator.

Ellen Johnson Sirleaf, Liberia's former president and Finance Minister, is another individual who has a similar profile. She worked for the World Bank, and she served as the director of the United Nations Development Programme in Africa before she was elected president. As president, she pursued a "Poverty Reduction Strategy (PRS)" program, an economic resuscitative edict for third-world conflict nations seeking charity donations and grants from global institutions and Western nations.

Under Sirleaf, Liberia received $16 billion in aid and donations and $5 billion in debt relief. Aid also covered the cost of security and defense, and up to 60% of her government budget. It allowed her to quadruple her pay and compensation as president several hundred times. She offered similar pay and compensation increases to the lawmakers to pass the measure into law.

Her administration's poor management practices went as far as classifying the repairs and constructions of schools, clinics, and roads as investments rather than development. In the end, her government was plagued by corruption, nepotism, huge income disparity, high unemployment, poor fiscal policy and mismanagement, and stagnant economic growth.

The economy fluctuated between -1.6% and 8% growth, driven primarily by rent, the presence and operations of the UN, charitable organizations, their activities, and donations. After she left office in 2018, charity donations and foreign begging dried up; her successor had to fund his own defense and security. Economic growth also never exceeded 5% under her successor's administrations. The short- and long-term impacts of her catastrophic policy failure will continue to wreak havoc on the country until some of her actions are reversed.

The PRS program also failed despite being backed by a substantial lobbying effort in Washington, D.C., and employing the expertise of prominent figures such as Paul Collier, Tony Blair, Jeffrey Sachs, and Bill Clinton.

In contrast, indigenous programs and policies observed tend to work better for the country than those prescribed by global institutions and foreign lobbyists. For instance, the work, policies, and performance of Sanusi Lamido Sanusi, the former Central Bank Governor of Nigeria, and Stephen Tolbert, the former Finance Minister of Liberia, had a positive impact on their countries' economies, occasionally opposing the directives of the World Bank and the IMF. Neither man worked for those institutions, but their policies were effective for their respective nations.

Furthermore, under Charles Taylor's administration, when the country faced crippling sanctions and embargoes, Liberia grew 106.28% in 1997, according to the World Bank.

Taylor did not follow Sirleaf's approach, nor adhere to the World Bank or the IMF programs. Despite economic sanctions and the withdrawal of aid, he maintained a double-digit growth rate until his ousting in 2003.

For countries like Liberia to prosper, they must develop indigenous policies and leverage their local talents to take their countries where they aspire.

In conclusion, this manifesto recommends that Liberians adopt some of the positive traits, behaviors, and attitudes described above in their daily dealings to build a formidable and resilient nation with purpose.

Chapter 3:
Structures of The New State

Another reason for repurposing Liberia is to recreate the country as a District City-State aligned with its purposes and functions.

Under this system, the country will be divided into districts to replace the county administrative structure. In this District-City System, people living in districts will decide what happens locally in those places, not their representatives nor the president. They will choose their mayors and decide how they will fund and build their streets. They will also decide how to keep their communities and neighborhoods clean and select local officials to manage their affairs without the president or national government interference.

In the proposed District City-State System, the people will enact and enforce their ordinances, conduct businesses, manage their finances, and deliver social services locally as they see fit within the confines of the law with a greater degree of autonomy. So, how well a district does or doesn't shall depend upon itself, not the president or the national government.

How the current system classifies where people live and how their services, needs, and wants are determined and delivered is messy, disorganized, and confusing!

People live everywhere - in counties, districts, cities, villages, and towns, and their services or needs are not organized and delivered accordingly. Instead, the president is in charge of making decisions, overseeing defense and protection, law enforcement, services, street constructions and repairs, and managing these needs through the president's chosen county administrations.

Concentrating such power and authority under one individual has continued to confine everyone to the same fate under many different incompetent leaders for generations. Such a system is ineffective. It creates a flawed and corrupt resource management system and deplorable living standards. Few opportunities exist for those far away from the president, and those who oppose him or her can suffer severely. Furthermore, there can be no room for improvement and reform if the president disagrees.

This is why people in Zorzor, Harper, Gbarnga, and Robertsport suffer from the same worse conditions of unemployment, robbery, corruption, poor roads, and underfunded schools and hospitals as those in Monrovia. One person controls everything, and the same bad decisions are replicated everywhere. This shows that the county's administration system does not work well for the people and gives more power to a president who is not held accountable.

Even though each district and county has elected representatives and senators, the president is still responsible for meeting people's needs and achieving their goals, aspirations, and plans. A president must decide if a village has a school, well, or clinic. Without the president's approval, no county can get a court building or a new public works project. A single individual must decide and authorize what the people need and want, or whether a district has a street, aided by their family, cronies, sycophants, allies, and foreign interests or backers.

Presidents can use their powers and authority to pardon and protect themselves, their allies, and their associates. They can even use those powers and authorities to appoint election commissioners and reject the results their appointees produce.

The last two previous presidents used their powers to hamper investigations and prosecutions of scandals, corruption, murders, and embezzlements during their administrations.

As presidents wield such significant influence over the levers of power, any inquiry into their regimes is likely impossible, if not ineffective. However, the new district-city-state structure is created to replace the current system and establish uniformity across the board, shrinking some of the excesses of those powers and authorities from the executive branch of government.

The new system will also impose strong oversight over the presidency and dedicate the management of the economy to another branch of government. Some of the powers and authorities of the executive branch shall also be transferred to other branches of government to create robust autonomy at the county and district level.

Description Of A District-City State Republic

The District-City State structure automatically divides the country into districts that function locally without needing permission from the president. This new charter will also grant all districts the full corporate, political, legal, administrative, and financial power and authority to operate as autonomous municipalities.

This act will give full rights and privileges to any area that has become a district. This means that districts in Lofa County or Grand Gedeh County will have the same rights and privileges as those in

Montserrado and Grand Bassa Counties. They will not need approval from the legislature or the president to become a District-City or to use the powers and authority granted to them.

Such statutes will allow each district to function like Monrovia and Paynesville: to elect mayors and community presidents/town chiefs as local leaders, to make economic, financial, social, political, and legal decisions independently of other districts but in accordance with the law, and to enact ordinances as it wishes without meddling or needing approval from the president, directly or indirectly.

Under the county administration system, the current decentralized plan, and the local government act, the legislature must grant a district its status. Also, the current law is still based on county systems administered by the president.

For example, the Minister of Finance and three other central government officials are in charge of the "County Government Fiscal Boards" appointed by the President, according to the Local Government Act. Such an arrangement has no autonomy.

Furthermore, the county administration system has proven dysfunctional, inadequate, and expensive. It forces everyone to live under the same poor economic conditions set by the president, replete with dire consequences. These broken systems benefit only presidents, their allies, and unqualified politicians who are recycled in and out of appointed positions while hurting the people.

In the District-City State structure, the first requirement for reform will be downsizing, reshaping, and reforming the national government to establish autonomy at the district level.

Under this structure and system, the national government will protect and defend the country and enforce and regulate the law. Counties will manage resources, and local governments in the district will provide services to the people.

Next, the national government will be reorganized to perform and operate only regulatory, defense, national security, law enforcement ministries, agencies, and entities.

All other ministries and agencies that manage resources like land, waterways, forests, minerals, and infrastructure will be transferred to county governments and serve as intermediaries between districts, connecting them by roads, utilities, etc.

Agencies and ministries, such as the Group of 72nd, Gender, Children, and Social Protection, which offer services like adoption and orphanage management, as well as those responsible for National ID Card verification and disability benefits distribution, will be transferred to municipalities for management by their respective district governments.

The sixty-one State-Owned enterprises (SOEs), such as the National Insurance Company of Liberia, NICOL, Liberia Electricity Corporation (LEC), petroleum refineries, marketing produce corporations, and ports, will transfer into private ownership, managed and owned by Liberian shareholders. Some corporations will further consolidate and merge to form large, more robust companies to produce goods and services for local consumption and export, providing millions of Liberians with jobs and career opportunities.

Companies and agencies that provide public service functions, such as the Culture Ambassadors and National Museum will be transferred to and managed by the charitable sector.

———————

Unlike the current system, the District-City structure allows each district to receive its subsidies directly from the Central Bank, without intermediaries, based on certain percentages of the national budget outlined in law (the constitution) and controlled by the Central Bank.

The new system eliminates patronage and all entrenched corrupt practices that the president, senators, and representatives currently exercise over districts and counties. It makes annual budget passages by the president and legislature obsolete. Expenditures will be set in law by percentages and disbursed to recipients by the Central Bank without additional approvals from the legislature or the president.

Districts will not have to wait for national politicians to hand out funds before a town can build a road, dig a well, or construct a townhall. One district does not have to agree before another can make economic decisions or appoint an individual to office.

Each district shall thrive and flourish based on the decisions it makes. If they impose excessive taxes and enact harmful laws that drive away residents to another district, or govern their district well and attract people, so be it! The people, not the president, shall make these kinds of decisions.

How well a district flourishes or how badly it fails will depend on the decisions the people make, rather than those of the president or a political party.

Their overseas residents will also be empowered to participate in district politics, voting, elections, legislation, and levies with little or no restrictions.

Districts in Maryland, Bassa, and Lofa counties will have the same power and authority as any other district in any part of the country to enforce their laws and improve their economy and environment as they deem necessary. They will not have to suffer the same fates financially, politically, socially, etc., all over the country either, because their economies won't be tied together or be determined by incompetent presidents or administrations.

Michigan and its cities can be used as a case study to give an example of Liberia's proposed District City-State Structure. In 2008, Detroit faced difficult financial and managerial problems and had to file for bankruptcy despite its well-developed infrastructure and amenities, including paved streets, electricity, universities, and corporations. In contrast, its neighboring cities, **Grand Rapids**, Lansing, Kalamazoo, and Ann Arbor, thrive in the same state.

It's crucial to understand that the mere development of roads and buildings is not enough to sustain a city's life. These structures do not pay hospital bills, send children to school, or put food on the table.

As seen in the case of Detroit, despite its paved roads, corporations, universities, and skyscrapers, the city still failed. It's the employment opportunities, commerce, economic activities, and the banking system that truly keep cities thriving. These are the factors that Liberian presidents and politicians often ignore in favor of highways, roads to farms, and aesthetically pleasing buildings.

All the cities in Michigan did not fail because they were not managed, governed, and operated by the same management and local policies as Liberia's county administrative system reflects. Detroit operated as a separate city within Michigan. Its failure and mismanagement were restricted only to its geographical location. If they had all been tied to the same fate, they would likely have experienced the same problems and filed for Chapter 11. But they weren't.

This book advocates applying the same strategic corporate, legal, political, administrative, financial, systemic, and managerial approaches to the new district system! Allow each district to manage itself separately from the others. If a district or two within a county fails and faces economic and political hardship, it should be independent of the others. Instead of letting all experience or being subjected to the same adverse conditions due to the same bad decisions one leader makes for all.

Key characteristics districts will need to flourish are as follows:

- According to the basic district's layout, public amenities, and services, a district with at least one hundred thousand residents of voting age shall be ideal for stimulating considerable commerce, banking, financial activities, and economic, political, and social engagements.

- A district must have large land spaces for at least an airport, stadium, hospital, high school-college, factories, corporations, living spaces, etc.

- All residents (citizens and foreigners) will be required to obtain a Residency Identification Number (RIN), a bank account, and a phone number to conduct or engage in any official business with the State or district throughout the country.

- RIN will be required for employment, school, travel, bank account, obtaining official documents, law enforcement, and identification purposes.

- The bank account and phone numbers will be necessary for conducting financial transactions, cash transfers, and electronic voting.

- Districts will levy (resident) taxes to fund, operate, and manage their affairs and construct their roads, streets, and public spaces independently of the national and county governments.

- Districts will reintroduce and refine the Special Emergency Life Food demographic censusing system and the Ebola mapping program as models to delineate districts, establish a voting system, distribute services, and implement cash transfers, among other tasks.

The Current Problems and Solutions

The District-city system attempts to solve a problem in a country where the nation's structure is arranged to give an advantage to the president or a small group of people around the president, to the total exclusion of the majority. That sort of exclusion facilitates the unequal distribution of wealth and resources and perpetuates corruption and inequalities within the law.

For example, the District of Careysburg, incorporated in 1923, is the only district in the country with exclusive legal rights and economic privileges that no other district enjoys.

According to the 2022 Census, Careysburg is about 111,369 square kilometers and has a population of 55,000 residents. Careysburg is not a county but has a superintendent, mayor, and commissioners, all appointed by the president; plus, Careysburg has a representative elected by the people.

No other district in the country is awarded this assortment of political appointments made by the president or enjoys special financial and legal arrangements as Careysburg does within the law.

Collectively, these appointment positions receive more pay and benefits from public funds than similar positions in other districts. Those legal, political, and economic privileges have also made Careysburg the beneficiary of the Western Railway

Station, Mount Coffee Hydropower, and White Plains Water Treatment Facility, which no other district enjoys in comparison.

Although Grand Kru County also has districts whose presidential appointees have titles like District superintendents, mayors, and commissioners, like Careysburg, but without the economic and financial rights and privileges mentioned previously.

Furthermore, these localities are not legally registered corporate entities like Careysburg, Paynesville, and Monrovia, and do not have comparable economies.

Compared to Careysburg, New Kru Town has a population of 72,000 residents according to the current census and covers an area of 1.98 square miles. But, under current law, New Kru Town is a borough, the only one in the country. That exclusion within itself is *unconstitutional*. Plus, even though its population density is higher than that of Careysburg, it has no power to govern itself, set its own zoning rules, or enforce its own laws. Instead, it depends on the Monrovia City Corporation for services through a revenue-sharing system.

Furthermore, only the Monrovia and Paynesville City Corporations receive funding directly from taxpayers through the National Budget, between 1 and 4 million dollars, respectively.

The proposed reforms will obliterate these unconstitutional dependencies and discrepancies.

When a locality of a certain size within a county declares itself as a district, it becomes incorporated and immediately assumes all the power, authority, rights, and privileges of a city with no preconditions, whether from a president or legislature, as written in the current law.

Some places in the country are attempting to develop and improve their people's living standards, but the old laws and financial arrangements are impediments. Away from Careysburg, Ganta, and Pleebo, in Nimba and Maryland County, without any preferential treatment or favorability in the law, as Careysburg, are both thriving, busy metropolises.

Ganta has banks, businesses, an (unused) airport, ample land space for development, hospitals, universities, schools, a sizable population, etc., which are some of the crucial features the proposed new district cities will need. However, it lacks the establishment of large corporations.

Pleebo also has banks, businesses, two large corporations, and land space for development, but relies on Harper for sea and airport services, a hospital, and a university about 22 km away.

Harper City in Maryland County, too, already has an airport, seaport, university, hospital, and land for investments and development, but lacks a bank, large corporations, or large-scale employers to help the city thrive like Pleebo. Furthermore, Harper's seaport, airport, hospital, and university are poor and unproductive State assets, declining further into ruins.

Unfortunately, no state assets in these areas can be developed or maintained without the president's approval in Monrovia or funding from the national government.

What appears to be lacking in these cities is coherent laws, systems, and structures that establish the same opportunities locally everywhere, yet allow people to determine their outcomes.

Harper could become a major economic hub in the southeastern region, but this could only happen if the president in Monrovia allows it.

This manifesto proposes that every district should have corporate status and greater economic autonomy without presidential interference. They should have the freedom to set their own rules, enforce them, and manage their elections and voting processes to meet the needs of their residents.

Large, well-planned areas should be given the power to use new laws and opportunities to grow into great cities. They must be empowered to regulate and construct their modern amenities and services, such as banks, airports, stadiums, electric power, parks, railways, hospitals, institutions, large corporations, factories, etc., to support employment and better living standards for residents so that they do not travel far for jobs, goods, and services afterward, how they transform these districts into paradises or keep them as slumps shall depend on their ingenuity or stupidity, not a president.

For example, instead of traveling 45 km to Margibi's Roberts International Airport for international and regional travel services, a more convenient solution can be created in one of the districts in Montserrado County.

A 10,000-acre parcel of land in District #2, between Neezoe and Pipeline, could be transformed into an international airport to handle regional and international flights. The airport, large warehouses, plane hangars, stores, workshops, international hotels, restaurants, and conference centers could boost growth and development in the district.

People in Monrovia could reach the airport in about 20-25 minutes using a 10-lane highway. Residents of the district would not have to travel far for job opportunities. But Gerrymandering, the metrics used to configure districts in Liberia, omits key factors like employment and services that make districts convenient, livable, and prosperous.

One big problem with the Gerrymandering (population) method used in drawing up districts in Liberia is that its formulas do not consider hospitals, stadiums, airports, factories, and employment opportunities for residents.

Take District#8 in Montserrado County, which runs between 12th Street, Sinkor, and Lynch Street, as an example. There is no large hospital or large private employer in that district to care for the sick or provide job opportunities for at least a thousand people.

Residents must travel to Districts #9 and #10 to seek medical treatment at John F. Kennedy Hospital or St. Joseph's Catholic Hospital. Many must travel to seek employment opportunities and purchase goods and services elsewhere.

Gerrymandering is an old and ineffective system for Liberia purposes. Even the United States, which created it, finds that the political party in power draws electoral districts to favor its party, not the people. This is the exact problem the new system and form of government are created to address.

New District roles and functions

The Reformed District will now operate within these expanded roles and responsibilities. Under this new arrangement, each district will manage its affairs through the mayor's office, community presidents, and town chiefs. Each district will also have a team of advisors to interview and recommend candidates for local elections or appointments. After candidates have applied for the positions, demonstrated their qualifications, and are cleared by their human resources departments. Importantly, these actions shall be sanctioned and enforced by residents, not a president in Monrovia. This approach aims to foster an organized and active democratic process and environment within each district.

Districts Power and Authority

- **Enforcement Services:** This includes inspections, certifications, registrations, licensing, and permit issues.

- **Facilitate Voting:** Organize debates, discussions, and other relevant activities to enable residents to vote electronically in elections. This system allows residents to propose and vote on bills, referendums, bilateral and multilateral treaties, and enact ordinances, promoting a sense of direct democracy.

- **Maintain Legal Statutes:** File and keep updated the legal statutes that pertain to their areas, and regularly update their financial statements according to established fiscal guidelines and economic objectives.

- **Corporate Power And Authority**: Grant approvals regarding the powers and authority to make decisions, take on financial obligations, engage in legal contracts and issue directions within their districts.

- **Financial Oversight:** Maintain at least one designated bank to provide fiscal and budgetary oversight and various banking services. Districts must comply with their fiscal and budgetary policies concerning spending and revenue, which residents must approve through referendums, propositions, and levies endorsed by the bank.

- **Ensure Public Safety:** Each district must have a District Court and policing initiatives to support local law enforcement. Jailed inmates will be required to assist in cleaning and maintaining their streets and local areas.

- **Resident Identification:** Verify Resident Identification Numbers (RINs), phone numbers, and bank accounts for residents.

- **Plan District Landscapes:** Ensure that districts are surveyed and laid out according to appropriate engineering standards, zoning laws, and landmarks. They must approve the construction of buildings, cemetery sites, and other structures as part of development plans and regulations. Their funding and disbursement shall be tied to achieving these benchmarks.

- **Accountability for Cleanliness:** Hold mayors, community presidents, and town chiefs accountable for maintaining cleanliness and order in their districts by tying their pay and compensation to their performance. Marketing associations and their officials will be held liable for maintaining clean markets and selling areas. They will be fined and possibly face jail sentences if they fail to act.

- **Contract Services:** Contract maintenance services, road and building construction, cleaning, janitorial duties, sanitation, and sewage services shall be offered to contractors and small businesses within their districts. The district will require contractors to submit bonds when applying for construction and other skilled contracts. This bond requirement will help ensure that quality work is performed and will hold the contractors accountable in the event of any damages.

Transfers to the Districts

- National Food Assistance Agency
- National Identification Registry
- Monrovia City Corporation
- Paynesville City Corporation
- Ministry Of Youth And Sports
- Liberia Refugee Repatriation And Resettlement Commission
- National Commission On Disabilities

- Liberia Agency For Community Empowerment
- Ministry Of Gender, Children, And Social Protection

The New Form of Government

Within this District City State structure and system, this manifesto proposes a form of government in which the government is not the State, and the State is not the government, as the republican and democratic forms of governments worldwide have evolved into. Furthermore, the government does not own the land within this system. Instead, the State, or the people, own everything, and the government is designed to function as the manager of their affairs, periodically empowered through elections to manage the State and reflect the people's will and pleasure.

Like a corporation, the CEO and managers do not own the corporation. They perform a service in the company and leave when the shareholders decide or demand a change.

Therefore, the people will oversee the government to ensure it operates properly, within its power and authority, and to keep it in check to ensure accountability and prevent the misuse of resources. Such oversight will be different from what Liberia currently has.

This also means elected or appointed officials will only follow the National Plan and the policies the people gave them.

When elected, a president, for example, shall only regulate and enforce the prescribed policies and plans of the nation already created, not his or her own. They will not be allowed to campaign on fanatical ideas and policies.

Second, no public servants shall be immune to prosecution in or out of government, especially where the law is broken. Neither can those who oversee the government enact laws to set their pay and compensation, hold office for life, or protect themselves from prosecution as the legislature in a republic does. A few high-profile murder, bribery and corruption cases under two previous presidents are still unresolved.

In the future, it will be the Advisory Council that shall set up independent committees to investigate allegations and recommend prosecution.

In Liberia's current republican form of government, a few individuals are elected to represent the people. They control the State's resources and make decisions as they see fit. In a representative democracy, the majority is supposed to decide what happens through their elected leaders. However, in both cases, a small group of wealthy, powerful elites remains the country's permanent ruling class.

They are often in government, occupying elected and appointed positions where they can regulate and determine opportunities, wealth, and the country's means of production. That clique and their inner circle also enact laws and finesse the government in ways that disproportionately benefit them and allow them to enjoy the country's resources and live better lives.

Since assuming an appointed position in government in 1997, Edwin Snowe has moved to elected office and spent the last 20 years as a lawmaker-first a representative and then a senator.

As his wealth and living standards have increased, his constituency's living standards have declined or worsened. The recent leadership turnover in Liberia, Kenya, and Ghana also exemplifies those arrangements of the former political dynasties or second generations of the ruling class or political families, like Joseph Boakai, John Mahama, Nana Addo Akufo-Addo, and Uhuru Kenyatta, who are continually going in and out of government to hold power perpetually.

This charade of running a government in Liberia is no different from a monarchical system of government in which the king and the state are one! The king or queen owns the land and resources, and the people are their subjects. The monarch does as they please and does not rule based on the people's approval.

In all those examples, the ruling class is the State and vice versa; between the descriptions above and a state where an individual rules over everything, there are only a few states where some accountability measures are ensured.

People either adapt to their circumstances or rise to demand change, as Liberians have tried to do many times, but have not achieved the results they wanted. That failure yielded a military regime and other authoritarian conditions, as seen also in Myanmar, Burkina Faso, Niger, Mali, and Afghanistan; in these systems, the people are subjected to the rules imposed by the ruling elites.

Communist and Socialist states reduce public and private property to communal ownership in the hands of the unproductive masses. Their ruling class is also the State, which controls and manages all means of production, as seen in Cuba and North Korea.

In all these systems and state structures, the people seek alternative forms of government or states where power and authority reside with them, not their managers or rulers.

In a small, impoverished, and weak country like Liberia, the goal of this book is to establish a system that positions councils of civilians over the government (the president) to keep presidents in check and help shepherd other African countries in this direction.

Branches Of Government

After the reforms and restructuring of the current government, the national, county, and district levels of government will be created and designed to function through the following branches: Advisory Council, Central Bank, Executive, Mayoral Assembly, and Judiciary.

- **The Advisory Council Branch:** The Advisory Council Branch shall oversee the National Plan, government activities, and the conduct of public officials. Its oversight will encompass regulations, defense, national security, law enforcement, elections, and policies, ensuring that no president or administration can act arbitrarily or govern at will.

  The Council will interview and recommend candidates aspiring for elected positions, such as presidents, justices, Central Bank governors, mayors, and council members, based on specific qualifications for office.

  The Council will also interview and recommend heads of government ministries for presidential appointments, rather than confirming nominees the president recommends. It will also interview and recommend deputy subordinates to the principal heads of ministries and agencies for appointment.

The Council and the president will meet with foreign dignitaries, travel abroad, and represent Liberia to the outside world to prevent potential compromises involving the country's president. This branch of government will replace the Senate; It will not have the power to enact laws, determine its own pay and compensation, or enjoy immunity from investigation and prosecution.

- **The Central Bank Branch:** The president's current power and authority to manage the economy and fiscal and monetary policies, foster growth and development, and finance government operations, public services, and projects shall be removed from the executive branch and set aside as the Central Bank Branch of government.

The Central Bank Branch of the government shall be responsible for creating the financial conditions and economic opportunities for people to live better lives, rather than presidents and politicians. It shall also regulate and enforce fiscal, monetary, and budgetary policies and economic management of the State.

- **The Executive Branch:** The Executive, under the president, shall focus on defense, security, regulation, and law enforcement.

- **The Mayoral Assembly Branch:** The Mayoral Assembly Branch of Government will replace the current House of Representatives and become a unicameral assembly that adopts statutes, amendments, and constitutional provisions already approved by the people.

  Members will reside in their respective districts, where residents will determine and approve their salaries and compensation, and will only come to Monrovia for a few weeks to enact laws.

- **The Judiciary Branch:** The Judiciary Branch of government shall interpret the constitution, laws and regulations and manage its court system.

The Land

Under current law, the government owns all lands, and the president ultimately dictates their use. Presidents have used that power and authority to single-handedly award lands belonging to families and communities to foreign corporations and individuals without oversight, evicting thousands of people who lived and farmed on those lands for centuries. i.e., Firestone Rubber Plantation, and Sime Darby.

State Lands

In the new system, presidents will not exercise such power and authority. Most lands will be shared among the people, counties, and districts to support the country's growth and development. This includes land for homes, farms, business centers, factories, and roads. But parks, mountains, reserves, and unexplored mineral and natural resource deposits shall be designated state lands where no one can sell, mine, farm, hunt, or exploit.

Those lands shall only be expanded if a project(s) is deemed worthy of national development and approved by the court and the Advisory Council, not the president. This ensures that eminent domain and the right to use are fair and transparent, free of the president's powers and compromises.

The National Park Ranger shall have the power and authority to enforce and manage state lands.

County Lands

County Lands shall be appropriated for development purposes, such as railways, bridges, highways, ports, plants, plantations, factories, and corporations. The County government will appropriate and manage its lands, including the power of eminent domain.

District Lands

District Lands will cover the city limits, where people live, work, and send their children to school. It will cover their streets, buildings, shopping centers, theme and recreational parks, sports complexes, cemeteries, etc. These lands shall come under district control, including eminent domain.

Communal/Town Lands

Communal/Town Lands will include ritual and customs practice sites set aside for towns' use. The towns will own these lands and do with them as they please. County governments shall designate and set aside these lands for the people.

Individual lands

Individual lands include residential lands, farms, and private plots owned and managed by individuals. Each district, not the national or county government, will control these lands. However, selling land to foreign and naturalized residents will be limited to residential properties and commercial sites, with additional restrictions.

A Lands Released program will be created, primarily geared towards individuals and families to own land, accompanied by appropriate legislation, like a *Homestead Act*, to make it easier for them to access and own land. The law will also make it easier for Liberians to build on those lands, monetize their properties, and pass them down to their next of kin.

It will include provisions requiring natural mineral resources on these lands to belong to their owners, except those acquired by foreigners and naturalized citizens. This act will bar foreign individuals and entities from mining minerals in the country or holding a majority stake in mining concessions.

Finally, Counties and Districts, not the national government, will survey, manage, regulate, monetize, transfer, and tax their respective lands and properties. Under that same law, counties and Districts must make the appropriate land prices, fees, and taxes public under their respective jurisdictions. Both counties and districts can use that system to sell land and raise revenue.

The People

One key objective of this reform is to ensure that Liberians live a better standard of living and become wealthy. To do that, each citizen shall be eligible for state benefits funded by the Central Bank Branch of Government, which is not guaranteed anywhere in the current constitution.

The following shall include:

- Educational Vouchers per individual for students to attend a school or university or acquire a skill of choice. It shall be the responsibility of the Education system to ensure that Liberians obtain either a degree or vocational skills by the age of 20 and are ready for employment.

- Healthcare Insurance Premium per person to seek care at a hospital or clinic of choice.

- The Legal Representation Fee is paid to an accused to select their defense of choice in criminal cases.

- Cash Transfers and Dividends are paid to individuals, the elderly, children, and people with disabilities who are eligible.

- Acquire majority stakes in the privatized corporations and large companies within the country.

Other rights and privileges:

- Polygamy, like Monogamy, shall be recognized and constitutional.

- Voting shall be mandatory, beginning at age 16, organized electronically, and administered by the Districts.

- Residents of each District will be eligible to vote on bills, levies, referendums, and propositions in their districts, including electing and recalling elected officials and approving treaties.

- Twenty-five years shall be the minimum age to run for public office, and seventy-five shall be set for retirement or exiting from public positions or services, including the presidency.

- Service in an elected office or position cannot exceed two terms, 10 years, or the passing of the age of 75.

- Citizens and naturalized persons between the ages of 16 and 50 will be required to perform two years of National Service through the National Service Corps (NSC). Completing National Service shall be a prerequisite for public service and employment.

- A naturalized person meeting specific qualifications shall be eligible to work in the district and county governments.

Traditional Kingdom System

Parallel to the Advisory Council, and within the shadow of the State, there shall be the (Restored) Traditional Kingdom System. The titles of Paramount and clan chiefs' roles and functions shall merge and be replaced by Traditional Kings, who shall function on a regional level.

The Kings shall serve as the Heads and the Custodians of the nation's traditions, customs, history, rites, and ceremonies. They shall also preside over traditional learning and their institutions, i.e., poro and sande societies. Their roles, functions, and responsibilities shall include reconciling the peace, settling regional and tribal disputes, and building national traditional cohesion.

The decrees and proclamations of the Kings shall be legal, binding by law, and enforceable under the Constitution.

The Kings shall be the traditional royals, and their titles, rights, and privileges shall be passed down through blood lineage and traditional rites. No constitution act or amendment shall be enacted to subvert its power and authority and funding.

Merger to theTraditional Kingdom System

- The National Council of Chiefs and Elders will be merged into the Traditional Kingdom System.

The Economic System

The new economic arrangement, centered on a Wealth-Creating Policy managed by the Central Bank, is not just a plan, but a necessity. It aims to elevate Liberia into a prominent banking and financial hub in West Africa, a crucial step for the country's economic future.

The plan will ensure that these two main sectors are positioned to support technology, education, healthcare, aviation, manufacturing, construction, hospitality, real estate, tourism, etc.

The Central Bank, a key player in this reform, will be tasked with creating employment, raising living standards and empowering millions of Liberians to become the majority of workers and holders of corporate shares and stocks.

The banking and financial sectors play a crucial role in promoting economic growth, development, and wealth creation. This importance has led to it being positioned at the forefront of the reform efforts. They shall therefore be responsible for providing capital, driving economic growth, developing the country, and expanding opportunities in each district and county.

In Nigeria, for instance, Access Bank started operations in 1989. Several decades later, the bank is valued at twenty-five billion dollars and operates across the African continent. Throughout its growth, Access Bank has also provided dividends to shareholders and financial support for ventures and operations worth millions of dollars.

Imagine at least one Access Bank in each of Nigeria's 36 States, designed primarily to focus on the growth and development of each state, including the standard of living of the people, without interference from the president or national government. Such a banking system can also function like a cure for poverty and economic hardship in South Africa's townships and slums. That is the kind of banking architecture and financial system this reform aims to establish in Liberia and encourage other African countries to follow suit.

Doing Business in the Country

The reform also entails numerous steps to eliminate barriers to doing business in Liberia. The importance of creating and developing a business environment that fosters (corporate) growth and generates business opportunities in the country cannot be overstated, as businesses will be the tools unleashed to address the country's economic, financial, and social challenges.

The reform aims to achieve several key objectives: particularly the creation of more corporations and businesses to solve problems, offer shares and stocks, provide goods and services, foster growth and development, create job opportunities, enhance living standards, and generate wealth.

Special attention will be given to deregulation, eliminating the barriers and costs that currently make doing business in Liberia expensive, complicated, and time-consuming. This will involve simplifying the business registration process and reducing unnecessary legal hurdles.

Decentralizing business registration to each county or district, where applicable, and eliminating the cumbersome paperwork associated with the process is a key aspect of the reform. This could involve digitizing the process, reducing the number of required documents, and simplifying the application forms.

Counties that offer better services and lower rates should be allowed to attract more businesses. Second, reduce or remove some of the costly taxes and daily fees that entrepreneurs currently incur. Finally, explore additional funding options, particularly for Liberian-owned businesses, corporations, and companies, to access loans and grants in a more affordable and streamlined manner through the Central Bank.

Business registration should be a straightforward process, as obtaining a birth certificate for an individual. The process should be cheaper and accessible to the majority of people without requiring a lawyer.

Just as obtaining an individual's birth certificate does not require a lawyer to file or necessitate regular updates or annual fees, registering a business should not be burdened with such bureaucratic processes and costs. Suppose a business's existence can be confirmed through other means, like bank accounts, tax documents, and licenses. Should entrepreneurs still be subjected to annual fees to verify that a business is active? Moreover, aside from the registration forms, what does it actually cost the government to store the paperwork that justifies charging over $50 per registration?

In cases observed, a typical business registration can cost an entrepreneur up to $500.00, including lawyer's fees and a bank account. This raises the question: Why is obtaining a simple business registration so complicated and expensive?

The reform initiative also seeks to reform and establish a Tax Structure that makes national corporations competitive, funds government services, and supports national priorities. Limit the costs, time, and bureaucratic processes for starting and running a corporation for the majority of Liberians.

Key Roles and Responsibilities of the Central Bank

- Reform and restructure the corporations and make them available for privatization.

- Award incentives and funding opportunities to Liberian corporations to make them competitive in the country's targeted industries and sectors.

- Enact an attractive corporate tax scheme in exchange for increased wages, salaries, and dividends. That Act will allow Liberians to retain a greater share of their wealth, promoting financial security and stability.

- Stimulate growth and development by funding the government, supporting public projects, and investing in national corporations while enforcing fiscal policies and budgetary measures to regulate public expenditures through the Central Bank Branch of Government.

- Establish the printing of physical currency locally to exert control. Use Liberian currency exclusively to settle all payments in the economy. Expand the money supply. Add digital currency to the payments domain to cover person-to-person transactions, merchants, institutions, and the government.

- Amend the Banking Act to reduce the capital requirements for starting, owning, and managing a bank. This change will enable thousands of Liberians to establish their own banks and become shareholders, paving the way for them to become millionaires and billionaires.

- Fund energy and mineral reserves to support Liberia's economic growth and development and protect against price fluctuations.

- Fund the "sixty-one national corporations" to produce goods and services for the local economy, thereby creating jobs.

- Fund agriculture and food production through corporations to ensure at least ten categories of farmers and large livestock producers, ten per county, for the foods Liberians consume most. This differs from the current government's plan, which involves the government taking charge of farming and food production through loans from its foreign funders.

- Establish investment portfolios to fund and subsidize national defense and security, law enforcement, education, healthcare, and development.

Finally, instead of enacting new legislation and allocating millions of dollars to establish and maintain a national gold(mineral) reserve, the Central Bank of Liberia, rather than the president, will determine the quantity of gold, diamonds, and minerals that can be mined, retained, or exported.

In 2024, Nigerian lawmakers brought forward a bill to establish an agency to procure a gold reserve. Instead of creating another bureaucracy costing millions, lawmakers could amend the Central Bank of Nigeria Act to give that Bank control over gold and precious minerals reserves. That power and authority would regulate the quantity of gold and precious minerals the countries want to mine, store, or export. Such a strategy would secure the country's reserves, save money, and reduce bureaucratic inefficiencies.

The Defense And Protection Of The State

The primary mission of the National Government shall be to establish and maintain an army with a minimum force of at least 255,000 men, about 15,000 in each county. To act as each county's main defense and protection force, supported by the police, intelligence agencies, and the National Service Corps, constituted and trained by Liberians.

The Punishment of Heinous Crimes and Public Corruption

Crimes involving espionage, drug dealing, extortion, and public corruption involving amounts of $10,000 and above may result in life imprisonment, plus labor or the death penalty.

The death penalty shall also be reinstated to execute drug dealers, armed robbery, rape (of a minor), and (ritualistic) murder. In sentencing these offenses, the judges, not the president, will order the execution of the convicts facing the death penalty.

Furthermore, the court, or a panel of judges, shall be responsible for issuing paroles and pardons, not the president.

State of Emergency and Transitional Powers and Authority

During a state of emergency and transitions, the Council of State, as part of the Advisory Council, not the president, shall assume and exercise executive powers and authority and manage the country to prevent the president from using this period for any retributive or nefarious reason. The president will not make certain decisions, travel abroad, or engage in certain activities during that period.

In a presidential election year, the incumbent, his the executives, and positions which report to the president, must conclude its business, compile its reports, and submit them to the Advisory Council at least 30 days before the election.

The Council will audit and deliver this report to the new government as soon as the election results are announced.

Furthermore, the Council of State will hold full power and authority over the country for 7 days before and 30 after the national elections.

This arrangement ensures a smooth transition between administrations and prevents the sitting administration from manipulating election results or refusing to step down from office if it loses.

Immediately after announcing the election results or declaring the winner, the outgoing administration will start reporting and transferring all state assets to the incoming administration. Since the prospective candidates have been trained on the National Plan and the government's operations, the transition period will last no longer than 30 days. The Council of State will oversee the transition.

The Council will review all claims made against the outgoing administration and hire an independent counsel or law firm to investigate and prosecute any reports of wrongdoing, corruption, or abuse. It ensures independent legal actions and prosecutions against those who break the law, without waiting for a presidentially appointed committee to investigate and prosecute the president themselves.

National Media and the Press

No other sector in the country can better promote the nation's ideas and aspirations, as well as those of its people, than the media. This is why the media will play a significant and impactful role in the reform movement.

The media will take the lead in communicating the message of the National Plan, educating the public, and sharing the story of the new country. Therefore, the newspapers, television, filmmaking and broadcasting institutions must undergo reforms at both the district and national levels to dominate the media and press space, rather than relying on foreign press and institutions.

Like the reform in state-owned corporations, the media corporations must be larger and powerful to engage with the government, institutions, and individuals to fend off undue influences.

The media cannot play a subservient role to foreign press and institutions, especially those detrimental to the reform. Due to the potential wealth to be created and the seismic change to come, Liberian media cannot remain idle nor serve as a surrogate for individuals, government officials and private interests. They must be independent and dominating!

First and foremost, the media must be loyal to the country, as explained below relating to the Council of Churches. In pursuing the truth, generating profit, or raising concerns, they must prioritize and respect the ideas and symbols of the State that represent the new Liberia. In doing so, the interests of the country will take precedence over those of individuals, presidents, and private interests.

Their actions will not only help hold the reformers and the district-city state system accountable but also refine institutions, including the military, defense, and national security, as well as the traditional kingship system, and safeguard them against individual interests and foreign threats that could jeopardize the country's well-being.

National Belief And Society

The principles and ideas upon which the new Liberia is formed shall constitute a National Belief. This belief shall be rooted in the country's way of life, faith in God, culture, society, defense, history, etc. It will be the philosophy upon which the country rebuilds, develops, runs, and maintains itself. It will be the psychology of how it faces and overcomes challenges, competes, deals with allies, confronts adversaries, defeats enemies, and achieves its goals and objectives, like many other societies.

Every great civilization had a national belief or religion that helped preserve its way of life. It allowed them to worship God and uphold their laws, customs, and traditions in all parts of society. If they did not have one, they created it! Evidence of this can be seen in Egypt and China. The Greeks, Romans, Aztecs, and Mongols also had similar belief systems that still influence today's world.

In recent times, Islam has been the state religion in Saudi Arabia and many Arab nations. Roman Catholicism is the state religion in Rome. King Henry VIII replaced Roman Catholicism with the Church of England in Britain, or Protestantism. In America, Capitalism is the state's religion. Among the Chinese, Indians, and Japanese are also the beliefs in Confucianism, Hinduism, and Shinto, respectively. Their histories, cultures, social norms, economic systems, traditions, political practices, science, etc., are intertwined and embedded in their respective religions.

In Russia, the Orthodox Church plays a significant role in both the religious and cultural life of the country. It is often seen as a key element of Russian national identity, helping to limit outside influences. In contrast, the Liberia Council of Churches and its religious institutions do not demonstrate the same level of reverence for the country. After their commitment to God, they tend to show greater loyalty to their specific religious denominations and their overseas headquarters and founders rather than the nation.

In the United States, Capitalism is not just a belief system but the cornerstone upon which the societal system of government, law, finance, history, and way of life is built. Any other belief or religion that enters American society must align itself with the core dogmas of the "American Capitalistic" belief system.

Christianity, Islam, and Judaism are practiced in the U.S. but are influenced by its "capitalistic" economic, political, legal system, and tax rules, or are restricted. Therefore, independent countries like Liberia should work to develop and preserve their own belief systems that reflect their language, values, history, culture, and way of life. It should reinstitute its kingdoms, as seen in Ghana and Nigeria, as the repositories of its customs and traditions.

For example, spreading the *"British Bible"* in Germany, France, and Spain did not make those nations abandon their languages to speak English or get rid of their cultures and traditions. But in places like Liberia, the Bible has influenced and spread English's written and spoken language, not the Liberian reading and written language. Similarly, the spread of the Arabic culture, language, history, traditions, and practices worldwide has also happened through the conversions to Islam. The spread of the Chinese language is playing a similar role today.

As Liberia advances towards its enlightenment, foreign faiths and religions should be welcomed and practiced to the extent that they do not denigrate the local language, culture, values, and heritage as the Episcopal Church once did to the Vai's language, reading, and written script.

The public must establish a litmus test to determine whether foreign religions are allowed to enter the country or proselytize. One criterion for this assessment is to evaluate how well a particular religion or denomination treats individuals who resemble Liberians in the countries where that faith or denomination originates.

National Language

Following the approval of a referendum to adopt Vai, or Kpelleh, as the national spoken and written language, all public signage-including posts, street names, and signs--will be converted to the written national language along with English, similar to practices in Ethiopia.

As one of those languages becomes the national language, grade schools, high school-colleges, and universities will develop courses to teach it, enabling the language to be passed on to the next generation.

More national programs will be broadcast, and events will be conducted in the national language.

State documents, all forms of literature, textbooks, familiar words, and everyday objects will be translated into that language, starting with the Holy Bible. Whenever possible, commonly used words from other tribal languages will also be incorporated.

The State and Capital Names, National Flag, and Emblems

The new State and capital names, along with the redesigned flag and emblems, will replace the current ones within weeks after a referendum approves the change. These new creations must reflect a country in which everyone can feel represented. The new names of rivers, mountains, cities, and significant symbols must also reflect the ancestry of the country's indigenous people and the settlers.

In conclusion, these changes should be approved through referendums and outlined in the National Plan within the first five years before the next general elections.

Such a strategy will foster a new mindset regarding people's attitudes, cultures, and language that will now set the country on a new path.

Chapter 4:
Reforming the Current Structures and Systems of Government

The Executive Branch Reform

Within the Executive branch, some of the overarching goals and objectives for reforming and restructuring the current system are to lessen the appointing power and authority of the president and divest the executive branch of certain institutions and functions. The reform will also abolish the president's management of the judiciary, lawmaking, and the economy. Those powers and authorities spun off from the executive over the economy, judiciary, and services will be redistributed to other branches of government, creating a more accountable, efficient, and cost-effective government.

For example, the president's authority to appoint central bank governors, judges, justices, and the chief justice shall be abolished. The Advisory Council will interview and recommend judges to the Chief Justice for appointment.

Central bank governors shall also undergo the same process without a presidential appointment. In trade and concession agreements, the Central Bank, not the president, will negotiate deals and concessions approved by the people.

Districts, ministries, and branches of government will receive their appropriations disbursed by the Central Bank based on percentages. This act shall eliminate the need for annual budget passage by the legislature and approval by the president.

State-owned corporations will be transferred into the private sector, freed of presidential appointments, to drive the production of goods and services, employment, economic opportunities, growth, and development through the Central Bank.

Transfers, mergers, consolidations, cost-cutting measures, and reform tools shall also be used as the primary strategies for implementing the Reform Agenda.

Finally, the Advisory Council will oversee the president's powers and authorities, as well as those of all other branches of government and their officials, to ensure that these reforms are enacted without the president or any other individuals or public institutions obstructing the process.

The reform shall be structured as follows:

- All law enforcement, regulatory, defense, and national security ministries, agencies, and institutions will remain within the Executive branch.
- Ministries and agencies providing commercial services and performing regulatory and law enforcement functions and responsibilities, like the Ministry of Posts and Telecommunications and the Ministry of Transport, are split. Their regulatory and law enforcement functions and duties shall remain with the Executive, but their commercial functions shall be transferred to the private sector. Such reorganization will even affect institutions at the department level.
- Ministries and entities with similar roles and functions will merge and consolidate to improve, become more efficient, and cost-effective.
- The transferred ministries and agencies are further reorganized to cut the Executive or national government's costs by at least forty percent.
- This will entail reducing the pay and compensation of high-ranking officials, including the president, and lowering the cost and operation of managing ministries, agencies, and other overhead. It also means not purchasing vehicles, gasoline, and

scratch cards for appointed and elected officials and employees. They will be compensated well to buy and maintain their own cars, phones, and homes.

- State-owned enterprises, agencies, and institutions that provide commercial services, such as public education and healthcare, are transferred to the private sector. These corporations and institutions, not the president, shall be responsible for hiring their staff, managers, and executives and appointing board members.

- The Culture Ambassadors, museums, the ombudsman's office, documents, records, and archives are transferred to the charitable sector.

- The district authorities will take over agencies that provide local social and community services, such as disaster assistance and the issuance of residency identification numbers.

- Public agencies and institutions that manage resources are transferred to the counties.

Management roles and responsibilities at the county level will lead to developing and preparing future leaders for higher national positions. As more institutions and systems are established and allowed to operate independently at the county level, they will train and equip leaders with diverse skills, expertise, leadership styles, and perspectives beyond the reach of the presidency. This will create a pool of competent executives, managers, and leaders who are tested, proven, and ready to step into national office.

Presidential Authority and Appointment Reforms

After the initial transfers, consolidation, and reorganization of the Executive branch of government, the remaining ministries and agencies shall constitute the cabinet and fall under the president's power and authority. However, the president's appointment power will be limited to cabinet ministers, directors, heads of agencies, ambassadors, and high-ranking military officers (Major General and above), whom their human resources departments and commanding officers have screened and forwarded to the Advisory Council. After the Council's interview, they are recommended for appointments.

The cabinet ministers, directors, and heads of agencies will be responsible for appointing their direct subordinates, such as deputy and assistant ministers, deputy directors, and others, who will report to them. They (the cabinet ministers, directors, and heads of agencies) will report directly to the president.

Ministers and other high-ranking officers shall receive the names of their respective subordinate applicants for appointments through the same process. This arrangement limits presidential appointments, establishes a better system of selecting qualified talent, and establishes a clear hierarchy.

This will curb favoritism, nepotism, cronyism, and prevent the random hiring of unqualified individuals in key public positions. The new system also creates opportunities for the country's best and brightest minds to serve.

Screening and Interviewing candidates for appointed positions

Unlike the current system, where the president nominates someone for a position and the Senate confirms the nominee, the new system will require applicants to apply for the position through their Human Resources department first. Then, the applicant will declare their assets and undergo a screening process conducted by that department or the Civil Service Agency. Once a prospective candidate meets the eligibility and qualification requirements, their assets will be verified and confirmed by their District Bank (or Central Bank).

After the verification process, the names of at least the seven most qualified applicants will be submitted to the Advisory Council for interviews to evaluate their suitability for the position and their loyalty to the country. Following the Council's interview and assessment, at least the top three candidates will be recommended to the president for appointment.

Cabinet officials and ambassadors, including ministers and directors appointed by the president, will serve at the president's discretion. They can be suspended, replaced, or terminated at the discretion of the president. However, certain independent regulatory agencies, such as the National Election Commission and the General Auditing Commission, will remain part of the Executive Branch but will not serve at the president's command.

The president will not have the authority to appoint, suspend, replace, or terminate the chairs or heads in those positions. Instead, the president will appoint their officials, and they shall vote to elect their heads and chairs. These agency officials will then report to the Advisory Council, not the president.

Neither will Presidents be allowed to chair the corporate boards of State-Owned Enterprises (SOEs), serve as committee members, or appoint individuals to corporate boards or positions. To independent regulatory positions, particularly those responsible for overseeing and regulating the powers of the presidency. All of these powers and authorities will be abolished.

This change also applies to the heads of independent regulatory and enforcement boards, as well as civic regulatory agencies and organizations that require specific professional licenses for membership. Members and boards of directors of these professional organizations will be responsible for voting and appointing management teams, who will then hire their staff.

At institutions such as the Liberia Medical and Dental Board and the Liberia Engineering Board, it will be the members—not the president—who will vote for their board chairpersons and executive directors. Similarly, members of organizational bodies, such as the Central Bank Governing Board, the Advisory Council, and the Supreme Court, will elect their leaders among themselves, mirroring the operations of legislative bodies rather than being appointed by the president.

Elected and Other Non-Presidential Appointed Positions

Presidential aspirants, directors, committees, council members, county managers, and mayors fall within this category. They must first undergo the same screening process ascribed to presidential appointees above, apply for the positions, and be cleared by the Central Bank and Civil Services Agency(their HR department). Then, the Advisory Council will interview and recommend them to their entities or institutions' boards or the National Elections Commissions, which shall declare the individuals eligible candidates for elections or votes on their respective institution's boards.

Currently, anyone can declare their intention to run for public office or serve on corporate boards after being appointed by the president without undergoing proper screening. Candidates' competencies, characters, and the quality of their ideas are not adequately assessed and scrutinized. As a result, over the past century and a half, some of the most corrupt, unethical, and incompetent individuals have held public office, often due to their connections, wealth, or long-standing presence on the political scene.

The new process reduces the loopholes that allow such individuals to rise to public positions, influence, and responsibility. It will also serve as a more thorough and transparent process for electing or appointing public officials.

Additional requirements and experience for high-level public positions.

To be eligible for appointment or election to a cabinet position or any high-level public office, an applicant or political aspirant must meet the following criteria:

- Have at least ten years of experience in management, administration, or leadership.
- Completed the National Service Corps.
- Must have demonstrated exemplary character and reputation in previous roles.
- Showed outstanding performance in leading teams, administering policies, and managing budget resources.
- Have no history of misconduct, felony, malfeasance, corruption, or embezzlement.
- For the country's highest public office, presidential candidates must have

professional experience working in national or county government, large private business, or public corporations. They should have held positions as ministers, chief executives, directors, or leaders responsible for overseeing budgets in the millions. Their claims must be substantiated and verified by the Civil Service Agency, the Central Bank, the Advisory Council, and the Election Commission, which shall present them for elections.

- County managers, mayors, cabinet ministers, and other high-ranking public positions will require previous experience in roles and functions as supervisors, administrators, managers, or leaders, but less rigid than those for president.

- Under the new system, appointed officials and electoral candidates--especially those running for public office--must be cleared and approved six months to a year before campaigning or assuming office. To receive comprehensive training and instruction on the administration of the National Plan, the roles, functions, and responsibilities of the positions they aim to obtain, and the consequences of violating the law. So that when violators are caught and found guilty, they cannot profess ignorance and make excuses.

The Reorganizing, Merging, And Restructuring Of The Current Public Ministries, Agencies, And Institutions

I. Ministry of State and Foreign Affairs

The Ministry of Internal Affairs, the Ministry of Foreign Affairs, the Ministry of State for Presidential Affairs, and the Foreign Missions and Information Services Departments within the Ministry of Information, Cultural Affairs, and Tourism will merge to establish a new institution called the Ministry of State and Foreign Affairs.

It will be headed by a Prime Minister or head of cabinet, whom the president will appoint.

This Ministry will be responsible for national and international affairs, ensuring a comprehensive approach to governance. It will comprise two main divisions: the State Division and the Foreign Division, headed by deputy ministers appointed by the Prime Minister.

The Prime Minister shall manage the country's daily operations. He or she shall act on behalf of the president on international issues, functions, and meetings nationally under the directives of the president, who shall operate under the guidance of the Council of State.

The State Division will concentrate on domestic and national issues such as residency, borders, regulations, and law enforcement.

The Foreign Division, under the president, will address external and global matters, oversee diplomatic missions, and deal with international organizations to effectively represent and manage Liberia's image and interests abroad.

Under the new Ministry, Internal Affairs will be restructured and repurposed as a department to serve as a liaison between the national government and the county and district governments.

The Foreign Missions from the Ministry of Information, Cultural Affairs, and Tourism will transition to the Foreign Services, while the Information Services will become the Ministry's press office.

The Cultural Affairs and Tourism Department will be split into two distinct agencies: One agency will act as a regulator overseeing culture, tourism, museums, media, lottery, gaming, hospitality, and entertainment.

The other agency will recommend artists, writers, institutions, and organizations for grants and loans to the Central Bank to fund and support Liberian culture, music, tourism, museums, and media; their roles and responsibilities shall be to help make Liberia more visible nationally and globally. Ensure the publication of Liberian books, the production of films, music, and arts, and the upkeep of historical, informational, and cultural sites and attractions.

The Ministry of State for Presidential Affairs will be restructured into a Chief of Staff role with fewer staff and responsibilities. This new role will be dedicated to managing the Executive Mansion grounds and the president's office.

The Department of Immigration from the Ministry of Justice will merge into the new Ministry to establish greater clarity and coordination within the functions of the State Division.

The department will be retrained to enforce and administer the new residency law, welcome visitors at the country's ports of entry, and promote the image and aspirations of the "new country."

The law's funding and enforcement mechanisms will reorganize immigration services to manage entries, stays, documentation, and verification effectively.

As the new Residency Law comes into force, the Immigration Division will be responsible for enforcing immigration laws - the residency identification numbering system needed for most daily functions, primarily legal and financial transactions. This system will also significantly reduce the need for immigration officers to be present at checkpoints everywhere.

Currently, Immigration offices in some parts of the country are abandoned and in disrepair. The army and immigration officers have approximately the same number of active personnel, and these immigration officers are often stationed at checkpoints alongside police, drug enforcement agents, and revenue authority staff in remote areas, where they frequently harass travelers and extort money. But the new law will revitalize those offices in the various districts and make officers more effective.

To cut costs further under the Foreign Division, one ambassador and embassy will represent Liberia in Washington, D.C., also covering the United Nations and Canada. Another ambassador and embassy will be established in China. The same policy will extend to Russia, the Far East and Asia, the European Union, the Middle East, and South America. Similar reorganization and coordination will take place in the north, south, east, and west of Africa.

Embassies and diplomatic missions will also be streamlined to improve the management of the country's international presence and enhance overall efficiency.

This consolidation and reorganization of various ministries and departments aims to simplify and optimize operations, management, and costs within the new Ministry. All the merging ministries' administrative, personnel, transportation, and payroll departments will be streamlined.

For example, if 100 staff currently handle all payroll and hiring processes for the previous entities, that number will be reduced by 40 or more. The new ministry will, therefore, have 60 staff members or fewer responsible for payroll and hiring. Staff laid off during the transition will be relocated and trained in the private sector at one of the privatized companies.

The objective is to reduce the Ministry's overhead costs by forty percent. The savings will be used to provide staff with competitive salaries, acquire modern equipment, enhance the effectiveness of the Ministry, embassies, and diplomatic missions, and establish a State and Foreign Services College to train and develop personnel.

As the reduced staff focuses on the country's competitiveness, defense, and security interests at embassies, a new visa protocol will be introduced to streamline visa processing services to enhance efficiency, entry, and stay.

Visitors to the country will be able to first apply for a visa online and obtain approval before traveling. The application process will also require applicants to meet specific criteria and pay two sets of fees:

One will be their Healthcare Insurance Service fee, which will be determined based on the duration of their stay.

The other will be their Premium Legal Fee, which will be applied if the visitors come in contact with the law. If there are no incidents against the law, this fee shall be refunded upon the visitor's departure from the country.

If payment is made and the application is approved, applicants will be granted entry with a Resident Identification Number (RIN).

Upon arrival at a port of entry, immigration officers will register this RIN to confirm their entry into the country. Failure to comply with these regulations may result in substantial fines, imprisonment, and deportation.

Once visitors reach their district or residence, they must verify their RIN with the local district government, where their phone number and bank account number will be issued, which shall be the necessary and accompanying documents to the RIN for living in Liberia and engaging in legal activities or conducting commerce. A separate service will be created to serve the residency of diplomats and dignitaries in their districts.

A key aspect of this reform within the Ministry of State and Foreign Affairs is consolidating focus, alignment, and collaboration between internal and international affairs. This initiative aims to expand the country's strategic trade partnerships, agreements, and treaties, primarily in Africa, as its strategic focus. Its goal is to guide the country's actions and decisions, ensuring a clear and beneficial direction for Liberia that the people approve of.

II. Ministry of Defense, National Security, and Police

All security, defense and law enforcement entities will merge to form a new agency. The Ministry of National Defense will merge with the Ministry of National Security, Executive Protection Services, and the Liberia National Police to create the Ministry of National Defense, Security, and Police.

The new ministry will have three divisions: Defense, National Security, and Police. Each division will have a deputy minister who will focus on their expertise.

This consolidation and reorganization will establish a comprehensive framework for planning and executing Defense, National Security, and Police operations. It will strengthen the country's ability to identify and respond to threats effectively, enabling the seamless and rapid sharing of information and intelligence across defense, security, and law enforcement.

The Defense Division will concentrate on the country's military and protection capabilities, encompassing the Army, Air Force, Coast Guard, Special and Elite Forces, and the National Service Corps, all under the command of the Joint Chiefs of Staff, which reports to the president with oversight from the Advisory Council.

It will prioritize defense, protection, and nation-building. Rather than foreign corporations, these forces will lead the national design and layout of the country, as well as construction and engineering projects. They will also be responsible for building essential infrastructure, including roads, bridges, communications, airports, seaports, and security installations in key locations.

The strategy will also prioritize the recruitment, training, and development of the country's youth, equipping them with the skills, and discipline needed for the civilian workforce and enabling them to contribute actively to nation-building efforts.

The national militia, through the National Service Corps, will supervise and coordinate disaster relief services.

Unlike other governmental agencies, the Ministry of Defense, National Security, and Police will expand and receive increased funding to address the deficiencies in the country's defense, protection, law enforcement and national security institutions.

This funding mechanism will be mandatory in the national budget, ensuring the country is well protected and defended. This includes having barracks, training bases, equipment, prisons, and personnel paid well and on time. Appropriate arms, equipment, vehicles, planes, and helicopters are purchased and maintained. It ensures that the Defense and National Security College is established to modernize training and services in Defense, National Security, and law enforcement.

The Civil War undoubtedly developed and groomed many men into good soldiers, from whom men could be recruited into the army. These soldiers are already versed in guerrilla tactics, which many armies in the subregion do not have. Furthermore, they understand the terrain and tactical layout of the country. Such a talent pool of soldiers, generals, military strategists, tacticians, and training officers will be a proficient source for Liberia's purpose.

These diverse skills, talents, and backgrounds can be strengthened and disciplined, molded into a formidable army, defense, and substrate for nation-building.

The National Security Division will manage internal and external security intelligence under the Deputy Minister for National Security. The National Security Agency (NSA) will handle external security, and the Criminal Investigation Division (CID) will focus on internal security, VIP protection services, national investigations, and clandestine operations.

The Police Division, under the Deputy Minister of Police, will focus on law enforcement, public safety, and protecting lives and property.

Police officers will receive training nationally but deploy and operate in districts. Each detachment or district police command will be accountable to its district mayors and local leadership, who shall provide oversight.

The country will pursue training regimens and military exercises in Africa from nations and sources who closely mirror Liberian society, values, and culture.

III. The Ministry of Justice and Labor Reform

The merger of the Ministry of Justice and the Ministry of Labor into the new Ministry of Justice and Labor is a strategic regulatory and law enforcement initiative. This consolidation will create a more robust and efficient system, with the two main divisions focusing on the general rule of law, regulations, and enforcement.

The new ministry will include Labor Standards, Codification, and Litigation (Prosecution and Defense Office), and both ministries' administrative and Management departments will be merged and reduced. However, other departments from the Ministry of Justice will be reassigned to different ministries and agencies.

For example: The National Fire Service will be transferred to district governments, allowing each district to independently manage and operate its fire services department. Their national body will organize and coordinate common standards and regulations among various branches and overseen by one of the councils.

The Economic Affairs Department for Justice will be moved to the General Auditing Commission.

The Liberian National Police and the National Police Training Academy will be transferred to the Ministry of National Defense, Security, and Police. Additionally, the Drug Enforcement Unit will become an auxiliary of the police.

The Liberia Immigration Services Department will move to the Ministry of State and Foreign Affairs.

The Palace of Correction and Rehabilitation will be handed over to the County and District Governments. County Governments will be responsible for managing inmates on death row and those serving long-term sentences.

Inmates in county jails will participate in county road maintenance and construction projects.

District governments will have jurisdiction over inmates in District Jails. Inmates will be required to clean streets, parks, and public spaces daily.

The savings accumulated by combining both ministries from rent, utilities, fuel, vehicles, etc., will be utilized to train and adequately compensate staff responsible for enforcing labor standards, regulations, and law enforcement.

The new ministry will also review and revise the existing codes to make them more comprehensive and improve the litigation and enforcement process. Importantly, these consolidations will result in more efficient and effective public service delivery and responsible financial management.

The New Legal System

Under the new legal system, the practice of the judges (government) appointing public defenders to defend the accused in court will be abolished. Instead, legal vouchers will be issued to individuals accused of crimes and defendants in criminal cases, allowing them to choose their legal representation from private practice.

This law will apply equally to the government, which will require hiring lawyers from private practice for both its criminal and civil cases.

The Government and the defendant will receive the same amount allocated per case, and any expenses that exceed this amount will be the client's responsibility.

Foreign nationals who have paid their premium legal fees prior to entering the country are eligible for legal vouchers (bonds) from the authorizing agencies. For those who are not eligible, the ministry shall coordinate with their respective embassies or countries to meet the requirements and fund their legal defense if they are unable to pay as individuals.

An independent department, not the county or district prosecutors, will oversee the swift and fair adjudication and funding of cases before the national, county, and district courts. The ombudsman will also ensure that both the accused and the defendants have equal access to evidence and police reports, and that no party controls or restricts the evidence available to the defendant or witnesses for cross-examination.

When a lawyer takes on civil cases and wins for the State or government, they shall receive a portion of the judgment amount, separate from the fees charged or vouchers disbursed.

This proposed system eliminates the unfair advantage that government prosecutors often have due to their unlimited resources. It replaces an outdated model inherited from the West, which has historically been compromised and biased against marginalized groups and individuals, including the poor and disadvantaged.

Doing Business With Government And Public Institutions

All vendors doing business with governments and public institutions shall be required to list their goods and services, costs, warranties, and other relevant information online or on other digital platforms. This will allow for proper regulation, price comparisons, ensure vendor competition, and optimize service quality.

For instance, Toyota, Renault, and Innoson motor dealerships in Monrovia will upload details about their vehicles, pricing, warranties, and services to the platform, providing purchasers with various options.

If any corruption or misdeeds arise, investigators will be able to determine why a purchaser chooses a more expensive option over a better deal, why there is no insurance, or why there are delays, including the paper trail to facilitate audits, investigations, and prosecution.

This law will apply to all individuals, businesses, entities, and service providers offering products and services to governments and public institutions.

Each department within an institution, ministry, or district will directly purchase from vendors using the designated cost center numbers. This system is designed to track transactions, disbursements, and expenditures.

Bulk purchasing and distribution through the General Services Agency shall be abolished. The agency's new role and responsibilities will be to establish and regulate the purchasing platform and ensure buyers' and sellers' compliance with legal standards and requirements.

Before the institution and bank disburses payments, each transaction must involve the purchasing staff, department heads, and other third-party approving authorities. This is to ensure that each party involved in the transaction is held accountable separately during audits, investigations, and prosecutions.

This system of interlocking approvals helps prevent abuse, theft, and corruption. Additionally, all transactions will be processed electronically, making tracking purchases, waste, and instances of fraud easier to identify and prosecute.

It shall therefore be the official policy of the government to conduct business within Africa, amongst African countries first, before going outside the continent.

Dealing with Innoson Motor Vehicles from Nigeria, for instance, as the preferred choice for government and public institution vehicle procurement, will occur first before purchasing from Toyota Motor from Japan. This will accrue a host of benefits: As a large consumer of the company's products and services, Liberia will have the opportunity to establish a production and assembly plant, opens doors for investment, training, and the development of Liberian experts.

Holding Corporations and Vendors Accountable

(Foreign) Corporations, vendors, service providers, and contractors doing business with the State will be required by a new law to maintain between ten and twenty-five percent of their operating budget in a separate bank account locally, either in cash or bonds. This measure ensures that whenever they violate Liberian laws and incur fines, the government can easily collect the payments.

State-Owned Enterprises And Commercial Activities Reforms

The country's State-Owned Enterprises are underdeveloped and mismanaged. These corporations do not function effectively to serve their customers and provide better goods and services at competitive prices.

Most of the sixty-one State-owned corporations have failed and been left in disrepair. Of the twenty that operate and the government can account for, they must contribute to the national budget in addition to the taxes they already pay. Rather than reinvesting in their institutions to boost competitiveness, improve products and services, hire additional staff, and provide employees with better wages that reflect the cost of living, these enterprises have been structured to direct contributions or their profits to the national budget.

That approach sustains a wasteful system that pays high salaries to top elected and appointed officials. Ironically, a year later, these same officials reroute subsidies to these corporations through the annual budget.

The proposed reform aims to eliminate presidential control over public corporations and institutions by transferring them to the private sector. This initiative will allow these organizations to reorganize into competitive, large national entities that can produce goods, services, and jobs tailored to local needs. By enabling Liberians and workers to become shareholders and giving them the freedom to manage their profits as they choose, the reform seeks to promote greater independence and efficiency. They, rather than the president, will be responsible for hiring their management, staff, and board of directors, as previously discussed.

The Central Bank's next step in addressing issues within State-Owned Enterprises (SOEs) is to reclassify all companies into their proper categories accurately. Some regulatory agencies have been inaccurately classified as commercial entities, even though they do not carry out entrepreneurial economic activities. This misclassification has continued through multiple administrations, including Boakai's. For example, the Liberian Maritime Authority and the Liberia Electricity Regulatory Commission are both regulatory agencies that have been wrongly labeled as SOEs. This issue is explained in detail and discussed in earlier sections of this chapter.

The third issue is mismanagement. The National Insurance Corporation of Liberia (NICOL), which should be one of the most profitable and valuable state-owned enterprises, currently generates less than a million dollars in annual revenue and does not meet legal standards. Created by the 1987 Act, NICOL is supposed to insure all government assets and entities in which the government owns at least 50 percent. Unfortunately, Boakai and previous administrations have violated this law, as the corporation does not insure all government assets and entities, and the government has been subsidizing its operational budget.

Even with an apprentice management team, NICOL should be generating revenue comparable to that of the National Social Security Corporation (NASSCORP), which earns tens of millions of dollars annually. Unfortunately, NICOL is underperforming and will not grow beyond its current level under the present arrangement.

At the final stage of the process, the Central Bank will divest the government of all its shares and transfer them to the workers and Liberian investors.

The Central Bank will finance NICOL and all the rebranded companies, ensuring they produce goods and services for the domestic market, spearhead development and investment, and create wealth and opportunities for Liberians.

The Liberia Telecommunications Corporation (LTC Mobile), Liberia Telecommunications Authority (LTA), and the Cable Consortium of Liberia (CCL) will merge to form a larger, more competitive telecommunications company. The regulatory role of the Liberia Telecommunications Authority (LTA) will shift back to the Ministry of Post and Telecommunications.

This new entity will offer the government and customers various telecommunication products and services, including smartphones, internet access and cable.

As the dominant national telecommunications corporation, its main goal will be to serve the government and the public. This includes strengthening communication around the country's defense, national security, and law enforcement. It will also build and maintain a new national network and communication infrastructure for commerce, trade, healthcare, education, voting, etc, and provide goods and services at competitive prices.

The merger and reorganization will enable the corporation to secure financing from the Central

Bank and attract investments. This funding will support the expansion and maintenance of their network, infrastructure, products, and services across Liberia. By extending these services nationwide, the corporation will create job opportunities for thousands of workers and generate numerous business prospects.

Additional legislation will be enacted to support these reorganization efforts, ensuring that Liberians hold a majority stake in these corporations. Share purchasing schemes and profit-sharing programs will also be developed to benefit employees.

Previously, stocks awarded by (foreign) corporations were only distributed and restricted among top government officials, the ruling class, and their families. But, the new rule will give ordinary Liberians access to those shares and opportunities for investment in these new corporations, including shares in foreign-owned corporations that high-ranking public officials are currently hoarding.

Under the new regulations, SOE corporations will be prohibited from selling or transferring their controlling shares to foreign interests, individuals, or corporations. Foreign ownership or stakes will be limited to a maximum of 5 percent. Non-Liberians will also be barred from serving as chief executives, chairing these companies' boards, or making decisions on behalf of the company.

Allowing foreign corporations to dominate, manage, and operate the nation's telecommunications system, for instance, has created serious national security risks, threatened the financial and banking sectors, weakened government's controls, and threatened sovereignty.

The nation of Guinea bought out MTN Group Limited's control of its telecommunication sector to avoid that fate. The Guinean Government's action further reaffirms why foreign corporations shouldn't dominate or operate in these critical sectors.

This is the same reorganization plan this book proposes - to put the people back in charge of their country's destiny and control of its wealth. As a result, critical sectors identified where foreign companies and nations presently control will experience similar reforms.

Funding Former State-Owned Enterprises

The Central Bank will prioritize funding for national corporations to ensure they employ Liberians and produce goods and services for the domestic economy. The Bank will support these corporations in meeting local and regional demands. Laws will be enacted to strengthen and enhance the competitiveness of corporations and industries, particularly in sectors that focus on the domestic production of goods and services and employment.

The national goal is to help these corporations thrive, create jobs, generate wealth, and contribute to the country's development. This focus will especially target industries and sectors that minimize the reliance on foreign multinational corporations and imported goods and services.

The country will concentrate on at least twelve key economic sectors where its corporations must be competitive and dominant. The strategic approach to achieving this begins with investing in the banking and financial industries to make them the most competitive economic sectors. Next comes technology, education, healthcare, aviation, manufacturing, construction, hospitality, real estate, insurance and tourism.

As the Central Bank highlights investments in these sectors, small and medium-sized businesses and entrepreneurs will benefit from concept development, financing, and expansion. The Bank will pay special attention to Liberian startups and ventures.

Training Business Leaders, CEOs, and Top Managers
A Top-tier Accelerated Executive MBA education and training program will be established to train and support the privatization process. This initiative aims to specialize in developing and preparing young lawyers and individuals with advanced degrees to become the business leaders,

CEOs, and top managers at these newly privatized corporations.

The program will focus on positioning the country's private sector at the forefront of innovation, competition, problem-solving, and advancement. It will ensure these business leaders, CEOs, and top managers learn and demonstrate the skills to lead and dominate the economy. Drive the domestic market, produce goods and services, and create jobs, all while enhancing shareholders' value.

Other Commercial Entities Transfers

The Liberia Football Association will reestablish itself as an independent regulatory organization funded by its members (teams, athletes, investors, etc.). It will regulate and enforce rules across competitive sports, including teams, athletes, investors, and sports organizations nationwide. Likewise, entities like the Liberian Athletic Association will evolve into member-based organizations to regulate and enforce rules amongst their members.

The Liberia Football Association and private team owners shall organize, manage, and own the National County Sports Meets, Division Qualifier Leagues, and National League championships in all sports. They, not the president or the national government, will be responsible for the operations and management of these sports and business activities.

The Lone Star Brand will function as a competitive national sports corporation. Lone Star will organize and prepare athletes and teams to represent Liberia in regional and global competitions across all sports. The organization will offer equity stakes in its business, seek sponsorships, and sell tickets, merchandise, and more.

Lone Star will receive a designated allocation from the national budget to subsidize its activities and competitive sports, which the Central Bank will disburse.

All public stadiums and sports arenas will be privatized and managed by Liberian corporations and management groups. This will provide unique opportunities for these new owners to host competitions and participate in leagues regularly. The new owners will maintain occupancy, ensure profitability, and address maintenance, repair, and staffing needs.

Each county and district will construct its stadiums, which will be managed by a private company, further empowering the sports sector.

The government currently manages Samuel K. Doe Stadium, but it remains underutilized and in disrepair. The surrounding land is being encroached upon and littered with trash, and the government and its management team have failed to maintain the stadium structure and services effectively. Private management and ownership will do a better job!

Strong Independent Media

The fifth essential element of the reform is the media. The role of the Liberian media will be to support the Ideas of National Plan, hold the government, institutions and public officials accountable, and raise awareness among citizens. In addition to privatizing the Liberian Broadcasting Corporation, new legislation will prohibit government ownership of media outlets. This act includes strategic measures designed to ensure that Liberia's media institutions are large, independent, and robust. Specifically, it guarantees that Liberia's airwaves and national narrative are not controlled or dominated by foreign media.

National Charitable Organization Reforms

Organizations such as the Liberian Cultural Ambassadors will transfer to the charitable sector. They will establish their management teams and boards of directors, not the president.

Charitable organizations with a commercial arm will be required to generate at least 50% of their funding through their products and services, fundraising, and donations. The Central Bank will fund the other half.

The Group of 72nd will be transferred to the District Government level to organize and set up individuals who need assistance, paid through their District Banks.

*Specific regulations will be issued through the Central Bank to control the number of foreign charitable organizations allowed to operate in the country and the sectors in which they can engage.

Airports And Seaports

Airport and seaport reforms will be carried out in several phases:

First, the Central Bank will merge the Liberia Maritime Authority (LiMA), the National Port Authority (NPA), and the Liberia Airport Authority (LAA) into a single corporate entity responsible for operating and managing the country's harbors and airports.

Their regulatory and law enforcement arms will be transferred to the Executive, while their commercial functions will remain private. Their combined resources will be used to construct, operate, and modernize Liberia's airports and harbors.

This company will issue shares, generate revenue, and secure additional funding from the Central Bank when needed. It establishes a clear funding path to revamp these assets.

Then, management will focus on streamlining and consolidating business processes to boost efficiency and services. The Central Bank will require them to make their system faster, easier, and cheaper to clear containers, vehicles, and (capital) equipment, and make the ports more competitive within the region.

For example, replace APM Terminals Services with a port's complimentary application that allows shippers and customers to register and track their consignments without incurring additional fees.

APM Terminals does not operate in Senegal, Sierra Leone, or Egypt, where the service fees are cheaper and operations are more efficient. But, their services are more expensive, arduous, and unnecessary in the six other African countries, including Liberia, where they operate.

The regulatory functions of these entities, which were transferred to the national government to screen passengers, provide security, and conduct inspections, shall remain unchanged. But many of the customs fees or line items will be further reduced, if not eliminated, including bureaucratic fees and penalties, as well as challenges to businesses at the ports.

Next, the Army's Engineering Corps will lead the renovation of existing harbors and airports and the construction of new ones nationwide.

The newly established corporation will fund these projects, ensuring that harbors are accessible to ships and that even the most remote areas are reachable by air.

The long-term national plan for air transportation proposed aims to establish three major international and regional airports — one in each of the country's eastern, central, and western regions. Depending on local demands, a domestic airfield in each district will be connected to one of these regional airports.

Unlike the train tracks or airports, the country has five key harbors that require rebuilding, expansion, and management: the Freeport of Monrovia, Buchanan, Greenville, Harper, and Robertsport. As in the construction of airports, the Army's Engineering Corps, particularly the Coast Guard Division, will oversee the renovation and construction of the ports.

Then, a train track network system will link seaports to regional airports through county capitals to transport people, goods, and services. The plan is to establish at least one major stop in each county's industrial zone.

The Central Bank will then revive and invest in Liberian domestic air, land, and ocean transportation services to lower travel fares, increase freight services, and enable people to travel quickly throughout the country.

The new aviation sector will partner with Ethiopian Airlines in at least a decade-long program to acquire planes, train crew and technicians, and establish a national aviation system for civilians and military use.

After the first phase, their mentoring relationship will last for another decade until the sector can operate and function independently.

Streets, Roads, And Highways Construction

Each district will independently construct its own street and road projects throughout the country, while the national government focuses on highways. This initiative enables each district to independently initiate pavement construction projects using cement concrete, rather than asphalt, without relying on the national government.

Once a district has been surveyed, properly laid out, zoned, and planned, it will begin road and street construction using concrete cement from the Roads and Streets Construction Fund disbursed by the Central Bank.

Concrete pavement will enhance the efficient movement of people and the transportation of goods and services within districts, contributing to overall development.

Concrete streets and road construction are a more affordable and manageable long-term investment option than asphalt. They are environmentally friendly and abundant in Liberia, which can be cheaply and locally sourced. Furthermore, a concrete street will require fewer repairs, use less expensive equipment, and can be cast with average masonry skills. Maintenance and replacement of concrete surfaces are also quicker and more cost-effective.

Notably, the concrete street layouts in Harper, Maryland, from the 1940s, 1950s, and 1960s are still largely intact.

The country has an ample supply of limestone for cement production, as well as sand, water, and rock. This abundance enables the construction of additional cement factories, which facilitates the paving of hundreds of thousands of miles of concrete streets, roads, and highways in every district, eliminating the need for asphalt imports. The availability and cost-effectiveness of these materials will enable districts to efficiently pave their streets, both in the short term and the long term, at a reduced cost.

Additionally, locally purchasing cement and road construction materials will stimulate business, trade, employment, investment, and development. These activities will create thousands of jobs for local tradespeople, including masons, carpenters, technicians, engineers, and the development of experts.

Internet And Electricity Connectivity

The manifesto proposes providing electricity and internet access to all regions of the country. To support this initiative, a tax of 20% to 35% will be applied to all Electrical and Internet service providers, devices, appliances, and equipment imported into the country.

The revenue generated from this tax will be allocated to electric and internet companies to cover the costs of materials, equipment, labor, operations, and infrastructure development.

Once a home is built and complies with the standard building and electrical codes, it will be connected to the national grid.

Residents will not have to pay an electricity bill for at least a decade, incurring no additional costs during this period. However, non-residential institutions, businesses and government institutions will still be required to pay for their electricity usage.

For Internet services, users will benefit from reduced costs due to the imposed taxes. Additionally, free public access to the Internet will be available at libraries and designated public access points, especially during election periods.

Real Estate And Affordable Housing Reform

The National Housing and Savings Bank will reorganize to become responsible for funding the development and construction of homes, public buildings, hotels, national real estate, and infrastructure development at the national, county, and district levels. It will construct and develop real estate nationwide, offer loans, provide mortgages to individuals, families, governments, districts, and businesses, and maintain the landscape and properties where people can live, raise families, and work.

The New Housing Bank will develop homes for at least one million Liberians who are middle - and high-income earners.

In contrast to previous housing initiatives, where the Bank transferred estate homes to their owners without further involvement, this new program retains responsibility for management and maintenance with the Bank or a management company to ensure the properties and estates maintain their value for a small monthly fee.

The existing estates, such as Amilcar Cabral, New Georgia, Steven Tolbert, and Matilda Housing Estates, were turned over to their owners without a management or maintenance company involvement. As a result, these estates have become neglected and poorly maintained. Many buildings are in disrepair, and erosion has damaged large sections of the properties. Streets are damaged and dirty throughout the community. The grass is overgrown, and homeowners have built unauthorized extensions, reducing property values and the aesthetic of their environments.

To address the problems in areas like Old Matilda Housing Estates, the Bank will reclaim the management and maintenance of the properties. It will clearly define property boundaries and improve landscaping. After appraising the structures, the Bank will inform homeowners of their property's value. Both the Bank and property owners will have a few options:

1. The Bank can offer homeowners cash to buy their property. If it takes over the homes, the Bank will renovate them and make them available to a new owner, who will pay rent or mortgage, including a maintenance fee.
2. Or, if the homeowner chooses to remain on their property, the Bank will renovate the unit and charge a monthly maintenance fee only.

This scenario benefits both the property owner and the bank. Property values rise, and the neighborhood will experience improvements as well. When homeowners choose to move, they have the option to resell their property to the bank or another buyer, allowing them to pocket the cash from the sale.

For many landowners lacking the funds to develop their properties, a portion of the Homestead Act will provide private landowners with financing to construct commercial properties and rental homes. Eligible landowners will receive credit and funding from banks to develop and maintain rental residential units per regulations and codes.

The agreement between the bank and the property owners will ensure that the property remains in the bank's control until the loan is repaid.

After that, the properties will be returned to their respective owners. Such arrangement will require that property owners always have a hired maintenance management company to maintain the property. This law will also ensure that landowners don't lose their land and that properties don't deteriorate into poor condition.

Millions of homes, schools, universities, and public buildings are scattered in disrepair nationwide because their owners cannot afford the necessary repairs, and the banking system is not designed to address this problem.

This situation includes the homes of former presidents and public officials, many of which their families cannot manage or maintain.

The Ducal Palace Hotel, Housing and Savings Bank, Edwin J. Roye, and Hotel Africa are just a few public buildings that have also not been repaired since the war. Even thousands more damaged private and public buildings exist in districts and counties. Many of those properties are also constructed below proper building codes and regulations.

If the new bank partners with property owners to renovate, rent, and manage these properties until the loan is paid off, it would stimulate the economy, create jobs, improve their district's appearance, and increase the net worth of the property owners.

Education And Healthcare Reform

Until now, most reforms have concentrated on executive power and authority. However, this session emphasizes the education and healthcare benefits the average citizen should receive from the State. It examines how care and services should be delivered, how facilities operate, how training and education are provided, and how the entire sector is reformed, reorganized, regulated, and funded.

Unlike Article 6 of the Constitution, which states that access to education should be provided "to the masses based on available resources" without stipulating where the funds will come from, this reform explicitly places the responsibility for financing healthcare and education on the State through the Central Bank Branch of Government.

Instead of the government building schools and hospitals, hiring teachers, doctors, and nurses, and covering expenses for supplies and maintenance, private owners will manage these educational and medical facilities.

The Central Bank will finance healthcare and education through premiums and individual voucher payments, ensuring the sustainability and accessibility of these services. And the government's role will focus on regulating these institutions and enforcing the law.

Healthcare premiums and education vouchers will be disbursed to individuals to seek care, attend the school of their choice, or acquire a skill through service providers. Then, Liberian insurance and education voucher companies will pay the bills.

Funding will be obtained from privatized public institutions and hospitals, taxes, visitor healthcare premium fees, and investment funds dedicated explicitly for health and education. This funding will also come from sovereign wealth funds, and subsidies to support the sector's growth, development, expansion, and assistance for suppliers, vendors, and service providers to ensure that the healthcare sector receives essential goods and services.

Lines of credit will be made available to help Liberian healthcare corporations and proprietors develop, manage, and operate medical facilities and learning institutions. To electronically coordinate the transfer of patients and students (grades, reports, tests, and results) between institutions and facilities. In a financial crisis, the Bank will provide financing that can be repaid once these entities become profitable.

The goal is to build, renovate, equip, and operate facilities, transforming schools, universities, and hospitals into better institutions and advanced medical centers.

Students, their parents, and patients will be empowered to evaluate the institutions and providers that serve them. This review will form part of the credentialing approval and funding process, which will continually permit these facilities to operate or be shut down.

Liberian professionals interested in managing these new entities will be required to collaborate, form corporations, and operate collectively to become eligible for funding to take over those learning institutions and hospitals. As described in the mergers and reorganization section, they must also attend and complete the Accelerated Business Executive Program as leaders, managers, and business executives.

The Central Bank will grant any group of ten or more educators, managers, directors, doctors, and nurses working under the auspices of a corporation the rights and privileges to operate and manage large hospitals and educational institutions at the county and district levels.

Specialized service providers operating as limited liability companies or private entities may require fewer than 10 shareholders but must meet additional qualifications to be granted those opportunities.

Structural Requirements and Standards

Hospital and university buildings shall be designed at the county level to meet specific standards and requirements, while the designs of high-school-colleges, grade schools, and nurseries shall focus on districts, communities, and neighborhoods.

These standards will assess building designs, quality, population, proximity, and available amenities. Learning institutions, for instance, will have to include soccer fields, tracks, libraries, laboratories, and gyms.

The libraries in learning institution buildings shall be available for public use rather than constructing separate structures. Where they will be secured, guarded, and maintained.

District and county governments will regulate and license the construction of medical facilities and learning institutions to ensure they meet established standards.

They will also ensure that each district maintains sufficient operational schools within its boundaries and complies with specific spacing regulations. As part of the reform process, districts can operate one or two high-quality schools instead of four or five underperforming schools if necessary.

The excessive or insufficient number of schools across a district could negatively impact the quality of education, healthcare and business. Therefore, specific metrics will be used to determine the appropriate distance between the facilities and evaluate the quality of their structures. Additional regulatory bodies will establish guidelines for curriculum, testing standards, and performance metrics that schools must follow to remain operational.

Regulatory and law enforcement agencies are categorized as follows:

- **Facilities Regulations:** These agencies will regulate aspects of the physical environment of education and healthcare settings, including building structures, standards, water and air quality, and other environmental factors. Regulations concerning codes and structures will also involve the district and county governments.

- **Professional Regulation:** This group will oversee education, curriculum, books, training, safety, credentials, professional practices, disciplinary actions, testing, licensing, certification, compensation, standards, best practices, work safety and other related aspects.

- **Medication and Therapy Regulation:** These regulators will focus on medicines, food safety, disease management, quality of care, treatment options, monitoring, costs, payment, insurance matters, record-related issues, and privacy.

- **Equipment and Technology Regulation:** This category will regulate biomedical equipment and technology.

Medical Services, Training and Hospitals

In the healthcare sector, the primary strategy is to transfer all public hospitals and clinics owned by the State to the private sector to enhance efficiency and scale.

Next, a public university and a county's public hospital will merge, reorganizing into a University Hospital. For example, the Liberia College of Physicians and Surgeons, Maternity Hospital, Tubman National Institute of Medical Arts, Catherine Mills Rehabilitation Hospital, Dogliotti School of Medicine, and John F. Kennedy Medical Center will combine to form the John F. Kennedy University Hospital.

The University Hospital will now be responsible for building its own facilities, hiring staff, including teachers, doctors, and nurses, purchasing supplies, and covering repair and maintenance costs rather than relying on the government or the president.

This new hospital will synchronize care, specialties, and operations, organize its board of directors and management, and serve as the county's referral hospital.

Similar initiatives will be employed in each county to consolidate public hospitals and nursing colleges into new university hospitals to teach medical professionals, and equip the entities with skilled personnel without relying on foreign aid or non-profit organizations.

For instance, in Harper, Maryland County, the William V.S. Tubman University School of Nursing will merge with the J.J. Dossen Hospital to create the J.J. Dossen University Hospital.

In Bong County, Phebe School of Nursing, the Cuttington University College Nursing and Public Health programs, and Phebe Hospital will merge to establish the Phebe University Hospital. In addition to preventing the market from being saturated with doctors, nurses, and medical professionals, wages and salaries will remain competitive to keep pace with the cost of living.

These facilities will also be funded and modernized as referral hospitals for their respective counties. At the district level, funding will be allocated to establish at least a hundred-bed hospital in each district, managed by Liberians to serve local populations.

Unlike the Jackson E. Doe Hospital, which was built in an isolated location away from the community, these facilities will be constructed in proximity to residential areas, schools, district colleges, and factories, ensuring they are easily accessible to the public. Additional funding will be allocated to establish clinics, pharmacies and specialty healthcare facilities in communities lacking such services in ways that don't saturate the market.

The Ministry of Health's roles and responsibilities will focus on regulations and law enforcement within the healthcare sector. It will continue formulating, implementing, monitoring, and evaluating health system policies, plans, and standards across healthcare providers.

Other regulatory agencies, such as the Liberia Board for Nursing and Midwifery, the Liberia Pharmacy Board, the Liberia Medical and Dental Council, and the Liberia Medical and Health Products Regulatory Authority, will oversee different aspects of the healthcare services.

Education, Learning, and Institutions

Liberia's educational philosophy has traditionally focused on identifying issues like subject and verb misalignment and proper etiquette rather than solving practical problems, such as providing clean drinking water and cleaning local communities. The upcoming educational reform aims to transform the system into a hub for human development by fostering critical thinking, innovation, and practical skills development that can be applied and shared within the district and the country to solve real problems.

This reform will prioritize education outcomes, emphasizing problem-solving, nation-building, and nurturing a new generation of citizens committed to protecting and defending the country. The education and learning sector must be restructured, reorganized, and funded innovatively to achieve these goals accordingly.

Like the healthcare sector, all public schools, technical institutions, and universities will be transferred to the private sector and merged under Liberian private ownership.

The new owners, rather than the Ministry of Education, will manage all assets, personnel, and financial responsibilities, including payroll, repairs, construction, and supplies. They will be responsible for addressing research, meeting student demands, and appointing their own boards, not the Ministry of Education nor the president of Liberia.

This reform, modeled after changes in the healthcare sector, will reduce the Ministry of Education's size, roles, and responsibilities.

While the Ministry regulates educational institutions' standards and teaching methods, departments that once focused on testing, funding, hiring, compensating teachers, and managing school facilities and supplies will become independent regulators and management agencies.

For example, the National Board of Education, the Center for Certification and Accreditation, and the Education and Health Fund will be transformed into independent regulatory bodies.

The Education and Health Fund will be reorganized to oversee funding approvals and ensure that students and schools meet eligibility requirements and perform as required. While the Committee on Science Education will be established as an independent entity to promote STEM (Science, Technology, Engineering, and Mathematics) nationally through scholarships, competitions, and fairs.

The West African Examinations Council (WAEC) will broaden its scope to ensure that WAEC's test scores are utilized for college admissions and scholarship eligibility.

Several departments, such as the National Commission on UNESCO and the Monrovia Consolidated School System (MCSS), will be abolished.

Specifically, MCSS represents an inequitable and unconstitutional educational framework that does not exist in other regions of the country, thereby giving Monrovia an unfair academic advantage. Despite receiving millions in government funding, MCSS still performs poorly, with many of its institutions being uncompetitive and poorly managed.

Hundreds of private schools compete with MCSS, often providing better education while paying teachers moderately higher salaries. Allowing independent managers to take over former MCSS schools and making all schools and universities private would greatly benefit millions of Liberian pupils and parents.

This approach would foster competition among institutions, thereby determining excellence and the quality of services, ensuring that educational institutions, students, and educators all have a fair start. Furthermore, private schools tend to operate consistently, avoiding indefinite shutdowns and strikes caused by failures to pay teachers on time adequately, as public institutions do.

At the national university, lawmakers are on the board of directors at the University of Liberia. Yet, the university constantly shuts down due to underfunding, protests, and vandalism. Students are even learning in an environment lacking books, supplies, and well-paid staff. Worse, students and faculty face threats, intimidation, and abuse from officials in government.

Acarous Gray, a former representative and his gang trespassed on the university campus, abused students, and vandalized the institution's property without prosecution. The Executive Branch of the government in the past has vandalized the University's property, brutalized and even killed students, with no one being held accountable for these actions.

The proposed reform aims to make these institutions private and stops government officials (lawmakers) from serving on the boards of learning institutions. Establish strong security and laws for these institutions to prosecute those responsible for such violations.

The New Universities

The new education system prioritizes higher education to develop experts and specialists in business, banking, finance, technology, education, and healthcare, particularly in areas that address paramount challenges. Most importantly, universities will be designed to teach students teamwork, conduct research, offer courses and programs essential to nation building, and award only advanced degrees, such as Masters and doctoral degrees.

The new higher education objective is to spur critical thinking, problem-solving skills, and a sense of nation-building to propel the country forward. Their knowledge and competencies must focus on the country in ways that solve problems and drive growth and development. To graduate more bankers, financial experts, dentists, surgeons, psychiatrists, architects, anthropologists, engineers, etc.

For example, students can earn a doctoral degree or a specialization in Liberian cultural studies, residency law, government, the education system, and the economy. This initiative aims to develop experts who will instill an understanding of Liberian history, form of government, economy, and the National Plan and their relevance to the country's growth and development.

The first step is to upgrade each county's current college to a university, thereby accelerating the development of more master's and doctoral disciplines and degree programs at those universities nationwide. To lower the cost of obtaining an advanced degree, these universities will offer courses remotely from one county to another or the rest of the country.

Next, develop a core focus on educating and training students in Banking and Finance, as the country seeks to build a competitive edge in these sectors. To support this goal, additional funding and scholarships will be available to develop a strong pool of experts in those sectors, fostering long-term growth and economic development.

Every idea and system the country adopts or practices must be filtered through the University, then into business, government, schools, and daily life. This coordination will produce a national life that perpetuates and supports the "Liberian Way of Life" and dispels external intrusions, especially those intended to subvert the country's progression.

The New High School-Colleges

Under the new system, each district will establish a high school-college program that allows students to earn both a high school diploma and a college degree within five years. The curriculum will focus on advanced mathematics, reading, comprehension, writing, and a chosen specialty in one of four areas: business, technical/engineering, liberal arts, or science.

Students will earn a degree and professional certification in their specified discipline during their four years of theoretical studies in the classroom and a year of apprenticeship in the profession.

After completing a degree and training certificate program in business, finance, technical fields, or science, students can pursue their careers or further their education at a county university to earn a master's or doctoral degree.

The physical infrastructure of institutions such as Booker T. Washington Institute and William V.S. Tubman High School meets the standards and qualifications needed to operate the proposed high-school-college and accommodate the four specialties.

An institution of this magnitude and with all those amenities will need to be constructed first in order to be granted a license and approval to operate as a high school-college.

The High School-Colleges are categorized as follows:

1. **Business and Technical College:** Offers courses in business, banking, finance, accounting, and customer service for the workforce.

2. **Technical/Engineering College:** Offers courses in mechanics, aviation repair,

computer technology, masonry, and construction.

3. **Liberal Arts College:** Offers education courses focused on the arts, drama, journalism, writing, filmmaking, history, Liberian cultural studies, and related fields to produce liberal arts professionals.

4. **Science College:** This college offers academic courses in biology, chemistry, police science, mathematics, physics, engineering, architecture, aviation, and more to produce scientists.

The New Grade Schools

Grade schools cover 1st through 9th grade. Between 1st and 6th grade, students will learn only four subjects: mathematics, reading, comprehension, and writing. Education during these years is designed to equip students with the skills and knowledge needed to become proficient readers, writers, and critical thinkers capable of making meaningful contributions to society.

7th through 9th grade, students are introduced to more advanced levels of the subjects they studied from 1st to 6th: mathematics, reading, comprehension, and writing, plus an area of specialty they want to focus on, like literature, geography, biology, physics, chemistry, accounting, etc., or a career path they want to pursue in college or their future, and an elective (music, sports, etc.).

This choice will complete the six core courses required for graduation. Students will do these courses until they graduate from the 9th grade.

The system will also project potential career paths that align with the country's future and human development, and the strategy to avoid many students pursuing a profession that is not in demand, underpaid, and oversaturated.

Many graduates are in professions where they cannot find jobs or are underpaid. On the other hand, the nursing profession is oversaturated compared to the size of Liberia's health sector, and nurses are underpaid. Such a solution will solve that problem.

Kindergarten

The same scheme will regulate and fund early childhood education, as described previously. Kindergarten programs will help students begin to identify and recognize letters and numbers, and develop reading, writing, and comprehension skills.

Chapter 5:
Counties Reform

Reforming the Structures and Systems of County Governments

Unlike the current Decentralization Plan, this aspect of the reform transfers all public entities that manage resources (rivers, waterways, highways, bridges, land, and forests) to counties. The county structures and systems will also serve as intermediaries between districts, connecting them by roads, utilities, highways, and bridges.

Second, County Governments shall demarcate districts and ensure boundary lines. They shall ensure that districts are empowered to operate independently of each other, meet their benchmarks, and are held accountable. If a district is mismanaged or fails, it shall come under receivership under the county government.

Under the current system, since decentralization was declared, the people have experienced the reverse. More laws or actions have been enacted that allow presidents to retain the power to withhold the appointments of mayors, commissioners, and local administrators. If the president refuses to act or enforce any law at the county level of government, no systems and structures are in place to counter or compel them to act or be held accountable.

Under the current law, the president appoints five members of the Local Government Fiscal Board, a seven-member team. Additionally, while counties and districts generate revenue, the president can determine how these funds are allocated between them and the national government.

With the impending reforms, counties will generate and keep 100% of their revenue. The Central Bank shall disburse subsidies to counties if they fulfill their responsibilities, such as connecting every district by roads and maintaining bridges, rivers, and waterways.

Entities that manage resources, such as the Liberia Land Authority, Liberia Rubber Development Authority, Rubber Development Fund Incorporated, National Fishery & Aquaculture Authority (NaFAA), and the Ministry of Public Works, are transferred to the county government. They are further divided into departments. After their transfers, some roles and responsibilities will expand, and others will be merged.

The Rubber Development Authority and the Rubber Development Fund will merge to create a unified Rubber Development Authority tasked with managing rubber development and farming. This new agency will consolidate its payroll, human resources, and other departments to enhance its focus on rubber regulations and enforcement within the sector. It will operate in each county where rubber is grown and produced, functioning as a county department agency rather than a national government bureaucracy.

The Forest Development Authority's responsibilities will expand to include managing reforestation efforts and overseeing mountains, waterways, parks, and reserves. The agency will be granted the authority to carry firearms and arrest and prosecute individuals who violate relevant laws.

The authority will be divided into 15 units dedicated to a specific county. Each unit will be led by a county director, recommended by the Council and appointed by the Head of the Managing Board. These 15 directors will form the Managing Directors Board, establishing forest management standards, rules, and regulations. At the national level, the directors will elect a chair through a voting process.

Ministries and agencies transferred to the counties will adopt similar organizational structures and arrangements to efficiently manage the resources under their control.

One agency that may see a split or reduction in its departments or a narrowing of its functions to the coastal region is the National Fishery and Aquaculture Authority (NaFAA).

The marine fishery department regulating commercial fishing in the ocean is unnecessary in areas far from the coastline, specifically interior regions. Therefore, only the nine-county governments along the coastline may have marine fishery departments. Meanwhile, the interior county governments will retain the aquaculture divisions. Such reorganization removes redundancies.

The Ministry of Youth and Sports will be integrated into the National Service Corps, and the management of sports complexes, along with the sports complex itself, will be transferred to the private sector.

The following agencies and ministries will be reassigned to ensure they provide services to residents in their respective districts: the National Commission on Disabilities, the Liberia Agency for Community Empowerment, the Ministry of Gender, Children, and Social Protection, and the Liberia Refugee Repatriation and Resettlement Commission. The National Veterans Bureau will now operate under the Ministry of Defense, National Security, and Police.

Additional Functions and Activities for Counties

169

- Each county will have a management team, including a county manager, directors, and advisors, tasked with organizing, managing, and overseeing county affairs.
- Counties shall also regularly file and update their financial statements following established fiscal and monetary guidelines and economic objectives and goals.
- The County Bank shall oversee fiscal and budgetary matters, financing, and other financial services. This bank will help ensure compliance with fiscal policies regarding spending and revenue.
- If a county or district faces a budget shortfall, it can borrow from the Central Bank for a fee, provided it receives approval from its residents. This provision will also ensure that funds allocated for services, investments, infrastructure, and development are not redirected towards salaries, wages, allowances, or travel expenses.

Transfers to the counties

- Liberia Land Authority
- Forestry Development Authority
- Rural Renewable Energy Agency
- Liberia Rubber Development Authority
- Ministry Of Public Works

- National Fishery & Aquaculture Authority (NaFAA)
- Liberia Agriculture Commodity Regulatory Authority (LACRA)
- Liberia National Commission On Arms
- National Bureau of Concessions
- The National Commission on Small Arms merges with the Liberia National Commission on Arms at the county level.
- Merge the Rubber Development Fund Incorporated into the Liberia Rubber Development Authority.

Chapter 6:
Executive Branch of Government

The Presidency

Following the transfers, mergers, and reorganizations within the Executive Branch's structures and systems, along with the reduction of the president's powers and authority, expenses related to the presidency -- including salaries and compensation -- will also decrease, including the elimination of the income of the president's spouses as budgetary allocations.

Corporations do not pay the husbands and wives of their chief executive officers because their spouses are appointed to executive positions within corporations. Why should the country provide such compensation?

The goal of the cuts or reductions of presidential expenditures is to eliminate the need for additional allowances and apply the forty percent targets across the board. Personal expenses that presidents can cover as an individual responsibility shall be taken off public spending. Beginning with the president, pay and compensation codes shall be devised to cover at least four times the cost of rent within a district in order to keep pace with the cost of living. This change will filter from the presidency to other high-level public service positions.

The president's new responsibility will be to lead official government events at public ceremonies and focus on matters outside the country. The president will speak and act on behalf of the country in international affairs, consulting with the Council of State.

In foreign affairs, defense, and national security matters, for instance, the approval of the Council of State will be required before the president can order troops to be moved or engaged in activities.

This requirement is in place to prevent any president and their loyalists from making arbitrary arrests, intimidating opponents, and undermining the State's power and authority.

Ministries and Public Institutions

A benchmark of forty percent for cuts and reductions has been established across all ministries and public institutions as part of a restructuring effort. Reducing staff by that target, consolidating embassies at the Foreign Affairs Ministry, and transferring pension, Retirement Benefits, and Benefits for Former Elected Officials from the Civil Service Agency, for instance, to the National Social Security Corporation (NASSCORP), will begin to yield those cuts proposed. The elimination of the purchase of vehicles for public officials, scratch cards, and Residential Property Rental and Lease shall all come under the scrutiny of cuts, reductions, and restructuring.

Sample Of The New Executive Branch

Category I: Executive Regulatory & Enforcement Ministries and Agencies - The president will have the power and authority to appoint the heads of these ministries and agencies, who will report directly to them.

- Office of the President
- Office of the Prime Minister
- Ministry of State and Foreign Affairs
- Ministry of Health
- Ministry of Education
- Ministry of Finance and Development Planning
- Ministry of Justice and Labor
- Ministry of Defense, National Security, and Police
- Ministry of Lands, Mines, and Energy
- Environmental Protection Agency

- Ministry of Mines and Energy
- Ministry of Agriculture
- Ministry of Posts and Telecommunications
- Ministry of Transport
- Ministry of Commerce and Industry
- Merge the Ministry of Mines and Energy and the Ministry of Lands, Mines, and Energy into one ministry.
- The Executive Protection Service, the National Center for the Coordination of the Response Mechanism (NCCR), and the National Veterans Bureau will be consolidated and incorporated into the Ministry of National Defense, Security, and Police.
- The Liberia Institute of Public Administration, Mano River Union, and The Ministry of Information will become departments at the Ministry of State and Foreign Affairs.
- The National Disaster Management Agency will transfer to the National Service Corps at the Ministry of National Defense, Security, and Police.

Category II: Regulatory & Enforcement Boards and Agencies - The president appoints directors and executives.

- Liberia Institute of Statistics and Geo-Information Services
- Liberia Medical and Health Products Regulatory Authority
- National Public Health Institute of Liberia
- National Commission on Higher Education
- Liberia Electricity Regulatory Commission
- National Water, Sanitation, and Hygiene Commission
- Liberia Agriculture Commodity Regulatory Authority
- National Housing Authority
- Liberia Airport Authority
- National Lottery Authority

Category III: Independent Regulatory & Enforcement Boards and Agencies: Directors and executives are appointed by members and their board of directors, not the president.

- West African Examinations Council
- Liberia Board for Nursing and Midwifery
- Liberia Pharmacy Board
- Liberia Medical and Dental Council
- Central Agricultural Research Institute (CARI)
- National Scientific Institute

Category IV: Independent Civil Regulatory and Law Enforcement Entities - chairs, commissioners, directors, and executives are selected and appointed by their board of directors.

- National Elections Commission
- Cultural Affairs & Tourism Commission
- Civil Service Agency
- Office Of The Ombudsman
- National Park Ranger
- The Center for National Documents, Records, and Archives (manages libraries throughout the country)
- Consolidate the Liberia Intellectual Property Office, the Liberia Copyright Office, and the Independent Information Commission under the Center for National Documents, Records, and Archives.

Abolish the following:

- Office of the Vice President
- Governance Commission
- Law Reform Commission
- Monrovia Consolidated School System, MCSS

Chapter 7:
Advisory Council Branch

The Advisory Council Branch, created to replace the Senate, is not intended to make laws as the current system does. Its primary role is to provide advice, ensure accountability, and oversee the review of the National Plan and state issues related to policies and procedures outlined by law and the constitution. The Advisory Council Branch shall serve as the guardian of the National Plan, making sure the government and the country stay on course.

Unlike the Senate, the Council will not make laws. Their oversight roles and responsibilities will include the power and authority to ask questions, investigate, and closely examine how other parts of the government, as well as different organizations, agencies, and companies, are carrying out the National Plan, conducting business, and adhering to the code of conduct at all times.

There will be no immunity to prevent the Council from exercising its authority over other branches of government, public and private institutions, and public officials throughout Liberia.

The Council will work diligently to ensure that all other branches of government and public entities achieve optimal outcomes from the proposed reforms, policies, and national plans. It will review audit and evaluation reports quarterly and annually to identify opportunities for improvement, spot risks, and suggest actions the country can take to remain strong, competitive, and prepared for the future.

These reports will also verify whether the institution is adhering to the reforms, complying with laws, and operating efficiently. With direct oversight responsibilities over the executive, judiciary, mayoral assembly, the central bank, and other governmental entities, the Council will vet and recommend candidates for appointments and elections. It will also recommend individuals and entities for prosecution or termination when laws are violated, following thorough investigations if necessary.

On occasions, public officials have been accused of crimes, subjected to retaliation, economic sanctions, and travel bans - in many cases - without investigation or prosecution. This Branch of government is created to ensure that those kinds of allegations are investigated, findings are made public and perpetrators are prosecuted.

The Council will also adopt measures to protect public officials, presidents, and individuals who may become the targets or subjects of (internal and external) retaliation. This protection is crucial in cases where a Central Bank Governor disagrees with the World Bank and the International Monetary Fund regarding policies and approaches.

Under previous administrations, investigating high-profile murders, embezzlement, and other crimes was difficult, particularly those involving presidents. Presidents have the power to form committees to investigate their administration if they so choose, and they can disregard the committee's findings and refuse to implement the report's recommendations without being held accountable.

Samuel Doe appointed the Draft Constitution Committee in the 80s. After their work, he abolished or replaced the committee when he was not pleased with the group's report.

Ellen Johnson Sirleaf dismissed the Truth and Reconciliation Commission recommendations without redress.

George Weah left the country for more than six weeks, resulting in a dereliction of duty, and was never brought in line.

President Boakai elected not to enforce the Supreme Court's ruling regarding the House of Representatives' Leadership in-house fighting and was never held accountable.

Such abuse of Executive power and authority also included the suspension of the Election Commissioner and the termination of the Central Bank Governor.

Ignoring the Supreme Court's ruling in Liberia is also seen in the United States, where the country derives its form of government and governing theory.

More precisely, after the announcement of the 2023 election results, President-Elect Boakai hurriedly traveled to the United States without oversight while the transition was in progress.

The context of that behavior occurred in an environment devoid of law, investigations, security measures, and restraints, underscoring the critical need for the proposed oversight framework.

For a president-elect, it raises the question of what was more important: His trip to the United States or his preparation to assume the presidency.

Who determines the priority? Who pays for the trip and provides security, the president-elect or the taxpayers? Was he permitted to engage in discussions on behalf of the country as president-elect? From where did this authority originate? How does the country confirm whether he acted in his own interest or theirs? What steps and measures can the country take to assure accountability, lessen liability, or prevent such behavior and risks in the future?

Under this proposed framework, the Advisory Council Branch, not the president, shall be tasked with addressing such matters, establishing independent committees and councils, and ensuring the enforcement of their recommendations.

The composition, function, and organizational behavior of the Senate and the former Truth and Reconciliation Commission offer valuable insights into how to organize and define the roles and responsibilities of future councils, as well as what pitfalls to avoid.

This case study presents an opportunity to establish a structure that possesses subpoena power and prosecutorial authority to address the problems discussed above effectively. It also underscores the potential for producing high-quality work and selecting individuals with the necessary skills to serve on these councils. Future councils must also prioritize members' participation, attendance and hold them accountable for their absences.

To ensure the smooth functioning of the proposed framework, a General Secretariat will be established. This body will be responsible for organizing, managing, and coordinating the council's activities (human resources, payroll, purchases, records, conduct), including research, organizing reports formulation, scheduling meetings, and overseeing daily operations.

Council's roles, responsibilities, and functions will include:

- The Council will review how governments and public entities utilize the most current and effective policies, methods, solutions, technologies, and knowledge to remain competitive and address challenges. It will also ensure that management teams adhere to their budgets, rules, and regulations while operating within the law.

- The Council will receive recommendations to evaluate and recommend Liberians who have *demonstrated exceptional patriotism and national service* to receive **National Honors and Titles**. Presidents will no longer have the unilateral authority to select individuals and award them titles and honors at their discretion.

- The Advisory Council will focus on long-term planning, specifically the National Plan covering 5, 10, and 15 years, and ensuring that the goals and objectives of all branches of government and public entities are achieved within that time frame, producing the desired outcomes from these reforms and policies.

- The Council will convene annually to assess the National Plan's progress and challenges, evaluate the reforms that have been implemented, and revise the plans and policies of various sectors, ministries, and agencies.

- In many countries, legislators can serve on several committees. In this Advisory Council, each member will serve on only one council that aligns with their field or area of knowledge. Also, unlike some legislatures, members will not be allowed to decide their salaries or create laws that benefit them personally.

- The Council chair shall also serve as the default member of the ministry or agency they oversee when there is a tie in a vote.

Eligibility

- Eligible council members must possess at least ten years of experience in their respective fields and be members of their profession's guild or licensing organization in good standing, where applicable to be eligible to serve on the Council.

  For example, judges must be Liberian Bar Association members with ten years of law experience to sit on the Judiciary Council.

- The Advisory Council will consist of at least 13 permanent, specialized bodies, each with 15 members elected from each county. Members will serve for four years and can only serve two terms. But, if they are involved in corruption, bad behavior, or do not act properly, the council or people in their counties can vote to remove them from office at any time.

Advisory Council Bodies

1. Council of State (on State and Foreign Affairs, National, County and District Affairs, and Executive Powers and Authority).

2. Council on the Law, Constitution, Legal, Elections, and Judiciary System

3. Council on Defense and National Security and Police

4. Council on Banking, Finance, Taxes, Business, Employment, Insurance, Investments, and Competitive Advantage

5. Council on Health, Education, and Skills Development

6. Council on Planning, Buildings, Infrastructure, and Network and Development

7. Council on Commerce, Tariffs, Industries, Trade, Imports, and Exports

8. Council on Agriculture, Food, and Drug and Safety

9. Council on Media, Culture, Religion, Tourism, Sports, Gaming, Traditions and Customs

10. Council on Science, Technologies, and Inventions

11. Council on Land, Forest, Water, Energy, Power, Reserves and Natural Resources, Environment and Hygiene

12. Council on Welfare, Relief, and Public Service

13. Council on Aviation, Maritime and Transportation

*More permanent or temporary councils could be established to provide specific oversight, advice, accountability, and consultation based on need. Temporary councils and commissions will address short-term problems, conduct investigations, and dissolve after their work. These Temporary Councils will be created by the permanent councils based on recommendations, not the president.

The Council of State

Only the Council of State, apart from other Councils, shall comprise at least one of the following:

1. Former President

2. Retired Military General

3. Retired Cabinet Minister

4. Retired Ambassador

5. Retired Mayor/County Manager

6. Retired Business Leader/Chief Executive Officer

7. Retired University President/Professor

8. Retired (Chief) Justice/Judge

9. Retired Journalist/Broadcaster

10. Current General Market President

11. Current University Student President

12. Current Trade/Union President/Organizer

Function and Purpose

Within the Advisory Council, the function and purpose of the Council of State in Liberia are to act as the default and collective presidency that safeguards the country against coups and attempts at manipulation and subversion.

The Country first implemented a Council of State system in the 1990s to serve as the public face of the government. However, this new structure will operate behind the scenes to balance the president's power and authority.

In some countries, this system acts as an advisory body; in others, it functions as a consultative and legal entity. In China, it operates as an executive body.

Liberia lacked such a system during the deaths of William R. Tolbert and Samuel Doe, as well as during the removal of Charles Taylor. As a result, those overthrows were quite easily possible and responsible for swaying the country's policies and focus. It has also taken the country many years to recover.

If a Council of State and a National Plan had been in place, would those governments have been overthrown? Even if it were possible to achieve such a task, would the ability to alter the nation's policies and strategic direction have been possible?

Ghana, Congo, Iran, Togo, Indonesia and Guatemala did not have similar structures when their governments were overthrown, making it easier to remove their patriotic leaders and destabilize those nations. Libya, Haiti, Somalia, Syria, and Ukraine are still struggling to recover since their (visionary) leaders were toppled. They are nations that did not have such a system in place.

Today, Iran has a similar system in place, which is why destabilization has become impossible. Similar structures exist in Sweden, the Netherlands, Singapore, Cuba, and China, which can partly be credited for making those countries politically and economically stable. They make their countries' policies, growth, and development platforms predictive. That system is lacking in the United States, where the gyration in policies and governing theory are evident.

Despite the growth and deployment in Rwanda, Russia, and Burkina Faso, the lack of a Council of

State system makes them susceptible to being overthrown or destabilized. Worst of all, their policies, growth, and development agendas will likely reverse.

To sustain such protracted growth and development immune to external influences, a country must be gifted with a succession of patriotic and nationalist leaders who will not deviate from their predecessors' plans and vision. The probable occurrence in any nation is impossible. That is why a Council of State-like structure, backed by a National Plan, is required to serve that role. This is one of the only systems that guarantees those stabilities and deals with foreign meddling, as seen in Singapore, China, and Iran.

Chapter 8:
Central Bank Branch

The Central Bank Branch of government will oversee the country's economy, regulate and enforce fiscal and monetary policy, promote growth and development, provide financial services, and fund government operations.

Under the country's current public finance laws and arrangements, the president is granted the power and authority to manipulate, manage, and formulate financial, economic, and fiscal policies and systems. These powers include reversing budgets, reducing salaries and allowances, creating bonds, and arranging loans. He or she can also take necessary steps to ensure the government runs smoothly and supports development programs. These powers and authorities include negotiating with individuals, companies, and nations to acquire goods and services for the country.

However, upcoming reforms will alter this framework. The previous law explicitly prohibited the Central Bank from taking loans on behalf of the country and vested those powers in the president. The new law will instead empower the Central Bank, a branch of government, to perform those tasks.

This branch will possess the same authority and power as other branches of government and manage state resources without interference from the executive branch.

Unlike the central banks in South Africa, Kenya, and Ghana, which have shares owned by corporations and foreign interests, the Central Bank of Liberia will remain 100% state-owned, a similar approach to that taken in Rwanda.

The profits generated by the Central Bank and those from the country's sovereign wealth funds will be allocated to support cash transfers, subsidize healthcare insurance, education, and legal fee vouchers. These funds will also support the government, create new industries, create jobs, and provide other opportunities where applicable.

The primary objective is to help Liberians improve their lives by supporting local businesses, industries, and organizations instead of depending on foreign assistance.

Unfortunately, countries like Liberia cannot reach their goals unless they create and enforce the right laws to develop and utilize their resources appropriately. They will also be unable to achieve such a goal if they continue to rely heavily on external interests for revenue, industries, and employment opportunities.

This is particularly evident in Nigeria, where legislation favors companies such as Statoil, CNOOC Petroleum, Shell, and ExxonMobil to the detriment of domestic corporations, such as Dangote Petroleum Refinery.

Liberia can structure its financial system independently and without being beholden to these corporations or external interests, much like the approach taken in Germany's banking system.

The new system will consist of a network of district and county banks insulated from the global financial system to facilitate local and national banking services. Foreign banks in the country will be restricted to commercial banking services, primarily international banking services.

Second, borrowing from external institutions, such as the World Bank, the International Monetary Fund (IMF), and the African Development Bank, to subsidize government in exchange for liberalizing laws and markets and borrowing directly from those institutions' influential shareholders nations such as the United States, Japan, China, and Germany, to construct roads in return for cheap mineral resources, outside the orbit of their banking systems, work as a double-edged sword against borrowing nations interests.

For instance, if Liberia borrows from the African Development Bank and takes a loan from Japan to build a highway, it obligates the country to two loan servicers, but Japan benefits more from these deals. At both ends, Japan receives a return on investment and extracts auctioned natural and mineral resources. Third, Japan exports expensive goods and services into a weakened economic nation.

Such an arrangement or relationship creates a trap, a poverty cycle that developing countries can't escape.

Liberia's approach is to first design and deploy an interlocking and robust banking and financial framework to minimize the effects of external infiltrations and manipulations. To guard against foreign lending, uncontrollable interest and exchange rates, create goods and services to make the economy specialized, valuable, and competitive.

Legal mechanisms and devices should also be in place to accompany the reforms and prohibit foreign nations, institutions, consultants, and organizations from intervening, advising, participating in, or funding any aspect of the reform.

Reformed roles and functions of the Central Bank

- **Administer and Manage:** The Central Bank will regulate the national banking system and the monetary, financial, and economic systems. It will also regulate and enforce fiscal and monetary policies, mint (digital and physical)currencies, and promote economic growth and production. The Central Bank shall ensure budgetary discipline among the national, county, and district governments, public entities, and ministries, managing revenues, expenditures, and other expenses through various accounts.

- **Regulate and Enforce:** The Central Bank will regulate and enforce laws concerning financial services and banking institutions. It will implement regulatory standards and policies and approve various banking and financial products and services. Institute directives, regulatory measures and agendas for nongovernmental and charitable organizations.

- **Financial Agreements and Negotiations:** Engage in negotiations for credit, loans, contracts, and loan agreements on behalf of the nation, as approved by the people.

- **Interest Rates and National Debt:** Determine and set low interest rates and create national debt and credit to fund economic growth and development, supporting government, private enterprises, and the standard of living.

- **National Reserves:** Establish and maintain National Reserves in energy and precious minerals (such as gold and diamonds) to secure and stabilize the country's long-term financial position and development goals.

- **Sovereign Wealth Fund Management:** Establish and oversee the nation's sovereign wealth funds and other financial entities, ensuring that profits and rents are used to subsidize cash transfers, healthcare insurance, education, and legal fee vouchers.

- **Funding Government and Entities:** All government branches, institutions, ministries, and entities will retain 100% of the revenue generated. In the event of a shortfall, the Central Bank shall provide loans and grants as necessary.

- All public ministries, entities, and institutions must borrow directly or indirectly from the Central Bank. Separate and individual ministries and entities' accounts will replace the General Fund Account.

- Every transaction coming to the Central Bank shall have separate accounts against which corresponding transactions will be debited and credited.

- The Central Bank will also be the only institution legally required to borrow and repay loans from foreign institutions and governments on behalf of the country. Such loans shall not be exchanged for natural or mineral resources.

- **Economic and Infrastructure Development Fund:** Establish investment portfolios to fund economic and business projects, as well as infrastructure development, including healthcare and educational institutions, utilities, real estate, corporations, and other essential facilities.

- **Auditing and Review:** Periodically audit and review the operations of public entities to ensure compliance with relevant regulations and standards. Liberian auditing firms will periodically review and audit the Central Bank under the supervision of the Council on Banking, Finance, Taxes, Business, Employment, Insurance, Investments, and Competitive Advantage.

1. **Governing Board**
2. **County Banks**
3. **District Banks**
4. **Other specialty banks**
5. **Sovereign wealth funds**
6. **Financial institutions**

The Central Bank Governing Board

The Central Bank will be administered and managed by a Governing Board. This board is responsible for regulating and enforcing the policies outlined above. At the national level, this Governing board shall be the administrative arm of the Central Bank. It shall formulate policies and have general oversight responsibilities for the banking and financial sector, dealing with overall fiscal and monetary policy, interest rates, employment, growth, pricing, debt, liquidity, and risk management.

The Governing Board will consist of the 15 County Bank presidents, who will gather to elect the Central Bank Governor.

The Governor shall have the authority to appoint county and district bank presidents and other banking system regulators based on recommendations from the Council on Banking, Finance, Taxes, Business,

Employment, Insurance, Investments, and Competitive Advantage.

When a vacancy occurs for the Governor on the board, following the appointment of a new County Bank President, an election will be held to select a new Governor.

Key Responsibilities:

- Deal with National Debit and Credit
- Sovereign Wealth Fund
- Monetary and Fiscal Policy
- Regulations and Enforcement
- Economic growth and development
- National Reinsurance Portfolio

County Banks

There shall be 15 County Banks to prioritize their county's economic growth and development. To manage county finances, fund county governments, and make investments. They will focus on offering banking services and helping to fund corporations, big businesses, factories, and industries in their counties. The goal is to boost local economic activity, foster growth, and support development in each area through corporations and large businesses.

The County Banks will also regulate and enforce fiscal policies and public finance laws at the county level. They will provide banking and financial services to county governments, including payroll, transfers, credit, and other related services.

They will also provide capital to businesses and startups, as well as finance key industries such as roads, factories, and farms. The banks will support Liberian entrepreneurs and enterprises, such as Korto Momlu, Telfar Clemens, and Abel Grear, in developing corporations, manufacturing goods and services for export, and creating employment in counties.

For instance, the three individuals combined can create a corporation that designs and manufactures apparel, gear, and footwear for national consumption, including the Defense, National Security, Police, Education, and healthcare sectors.

County Banks will retain the county's assets, minerals, and natural resources on their books. For example, assets such as the Samuel K. Doe Sports Complex and Antoinette Tubman Stadium will be managed by the Montserrado County Bank, which will work to recapitalize these assets, enhance their competitiveness, and privatize them.

This arrangement ensures that strategic industries, national corporations, institutions, county governments, farms, factories, and manufacturing receive the necessary funding to provide goods and services in the market and create employment opportunities.

In the event of financial difficulties, the County Banks will leverage their authority to intervene, prevent bankruptcy, and help restore solvency.

Other Types of Commercial and Specialty Banks at the County Level

- **The Agriculture and Fishery Bank** shall finance agriculture, fisheries, poultry, farms, and food production.

- **Construction and Infrastructure Bank** shall fund public projects, including road construction, infrastructure, communications, utilities, and network construction and expansion.

- **Industries and Export Bank** shall finance strategic and competitive sectors, including manufacturing, as well as export goods and services.

- **National Housing & Savings Bank** shall finance the construction of public buildings, homes, hotels, national buildings, and projects, and develop millions of private and public homes and living quarters.

- **The Liberia Bank for Development and Investment** shall finance commercial ventures, innovations, startups, business product and service incubations, and the development and commercialization of goods and services.

Other Types of Financial Institutions

- Annuity and Investment firms
- National Social Security Corporation (NASSCORP)
- National Insurance Corporation of Liberia (NICOL)

*These institutions will primarily reinvest in Liberia's institutions, corporations, goods and services.

District Banks

Each district shall establish a District Bank to provide banking and financial services to local governments, promote economic growth by supporting small businesses, and offer residents personal and retail banking services.

The District Bank will finance the district government payroll, manage expenditures, oversee projects, and ensure sound and efficient economic operations. It will ensure that district budgets are strictly balanced and enforced.

Provide residents with checking accounts to conduct financial transactions and coordinate cash transfers and benefits from the State.

The bank will provide financial services, including money transfers, to individuals, businesses, and organizations both within and outside the country. It will also offer banking and financial services to companies that are officially registered in the district. The bank will fund businesses, construction projects, employment initiatives, and other business opportunities within the district.

The District Bank will also identify and invest in indigenous innovations and technologies — ideas, concepts, strategies, and inventions — that can be developed into goods and services to stimulate growth and create jobs locally.

The bank will conduct independent audits and review the district's financial and economic operations.

Local banks and financial institutions

- **District Bank** provides retail financial and banking services to individuals, businesses, and the government.

- **Community Credit Union** is established to provide retail financial and banking services.

- **Savings and Loan (S&L) Associations** that provide retail financial and banking services.

- **Liberian-Owned Private Banks** are established and owned by ordinary citizens.

Income and Living Standard

Part of the Wealth Creation Policy aims to improve living standards by increasing income to meet the basic cost of living.

Basic income will be determined based on the cost of rent; specifically, four times the rent in a district will represent that district's minimum wage or basic income. Other factors, such as economic growth, education, experience, profession, industry, performance, negotiation skills, and job changes, will also impact income scale and growth.

The calculation above divides income into four equal categories, each representing twenty-five percent of total income:

- Rent/Mortgage.
- Food, Utilities, and Clothing.
- Transportation (including car payments, insurance, fuel, or public transit fares).
- Savings, Retirement, Insurance, and Vacation.

At the macro level, the pay and compensation of the highest public official (the President) shall be no more than one hundred times that of the lowest-paid employee (a security guard).

Transfers to the Central Bank

- Bureau Of State Enterprises
- Public Procurement and Concessions Commission
- National Housing and Savings Bank
- Liberia's Extractive Industry Transparency Initiative
- Cooperative Development Agency
- National Investment Commission
- Agricultural Credit Corporation
- Liberian Development Corporation
- The Liberian Bank For Development And Investment
- Agricultural And Cooperative Development Bank
- The Lofa Rural And Commercial Bank
- ❖ Transform the National Investment Commission into the nation's sovereign fund, creating new opportunities for growth and prosperity.

Transfers to the Private sector -

Grade Schools, High School-colleges, and universities
- University of Liberia
- Booker Washington Institute

- Cuttington University
- Agricultural and Industrial Training Bureau
- William V.S. Tubman University
- Zorzor Rural Teacher Training
- Webbo Rural Teacher Training Institute
- Kakata Rural Teacher Training Institute
- Bassa County Community College
- Bomi County Community College
- Nimba Community College
- Lofa Community College
- Bong Technical College
- Grand Gedeh Community College
- Harbel College
- Sinoe Community College
- Forpoh Vocational Institute
- Grand Kru Community College
- Rivergee Technical College
- Pleebo Technical College
- Forestry Training Institute
- ❖ Plus all schools, colleges, and universities

Transfers to the Private sector - *University Hospitals*
- John F. Kennedy Medical Center
- Phebe Hospital and School Of Nursing
- Jackson F Doe Hospital

- J. J. Dossen Hospital
- ❖ Plus all hospitals, clinics, and health centers

Transfers to the Private sector - *Corporations*
- Liberia Produce Marketing Corporation
- Liberia Industrial Free Zone Authority
- Liberia Electricity Corporation (LEC)
- Liberia Petroleum Refining Company (LPRC)
- Liberia Water & Sewer Corporation (LWSC)
- National Housing Authority (NHA)
- Liberia Maritime Authority (LiMA)
- National Port Authority (NPA)
- Liberia Airport Authority (LAA)
- National Transit Authority (NTA)
- National Social Security Corporation (NASSCORP)
- National Insurance Corporation of Liberia (NICOL)
- Liberia Shipping Corporation
- Air Liberia Incorporated
- ❖ Plus all State Owned Enterprises
- ❖ Consolidate the Liberia Maritime Authority (LiMA), the National Port Authority (NPA), and the Liberia Airport Authority (LAA) into a single entity responsible for

operating and managing the country's harbors and airports. Transfer their regulatory functions to the national government. The combined resources of these three organizations will fund the construction, operation, and modernization of these assets.

❖ Merge Liberia Telecommunication Corporation (LTC Mobile) and Liberia Telecommunication Authority (LTA) to create a large national telecommunications corporation that provides goods and services.

Transfers to the Private sector -

Grade Schools, High School-colleges, and universities

- University of Liberia
- Booker Washington Institute
- Cuttington University
- Agricultural and Industrial Training Bureau
- William V.S. Tubman University
- Zorzor Rural Teacher Training
- Webbo Rural Teacher Training Institute
- Kakata Rural Teacher Training Institute
- Bassa County Community College
- Bomi County Community College
- Nimba Community College

- Lofa Community College
- Bong Technical College
- Grand Gedeh Community College
- Harbel College
- Sinoe Community College
- Forpoh Vocational Institute
- Grand Kru Community College
- Rivergee Technical College
- Pleebo Technical College
- Forestry Training Institute
- ❖ Plus all schools, colleges, and universities

Transfers to the Private sector - *University Hospitals*
- John F. Kennedy Medical Center
- Phebe Hospital and School Of Nursing
- Jackson F Doe Hospital
- J. J. Dossen Hospital
- ❖ Plus all hospitals, clinics, and health centers

Transfers to the Private sector - *Corporations*
- Liberia Produce Marketing Corporation
- Liberia Industrial Free Zone Authority
- Liberia Electricity Corporation (LEC)
- Liberia Petroleum Refining Company (LPRC)

- Liberia Water & Sewer Corporation (LWSC)
- National Housing Authority (NHA)
- Liberia Maritime Authority (LiMA)
- National Port Authority (NPA)
- Liberia Airport Authority (LAA)
- National Transit Authority (NTA)
- National Social Security Corporation (NASSCORP)
- National Insurance Corporation of Liberia (NICOL)
- Liberia Shipping Corporation
- Air Liberia Incorporated

❖ Plus all State Owned Enterprises

❖ Consolidate the Liberia Maritime Authority (LiMA), the National Port Authority (NPA), and the Liberia Airport Authority (LAA) into a single entity responsible for operating and managing the country's harbors and airports. Transfer their regulatory functions to the national government. The combined resources of these three organizations will fund the construction, operation, and modernization of these assets.

❖ Merge Liberia Telecommunication Corporation (LTC Mobile) and Liberia Telecommunication Authority (LTA) to create a large national telecommunications corporation that provides goods and services.

Charity Sector

Transfers to the charity sector.

- Human Rights Commission
- Cultural Ambassadors
- National Aids Commission

Chapter 9:
Judiciary Branch

The Judicial Branch, which interprets the Constitution and laws, does not manage its courts or appoint judges and justices. Instead, the Executive Branch has assumed control over the court's funding and appointment processes for judges, justices, and other jurists. Liberia and many other African countries duplicate this system without considering its fairness, independence, and implications.

That setup weakens the system and underfunds it, subjecting the Courts to the Legislature's and the president's control and influence.

During the House of Representatives' Power Scramble, the Court ruled in favor of the defendant party, but the Executive (President Boakai) refused to enforce the Court's ruling and was never held accountable, as mentioned under the Advisory Council Branch of Government. He even went so far as to provide his own interpretation of the law. President Boakai's interposition and invalidation of the Supreme Court's ruling are evidence that a change is needed.

In Brown v. Board of Education of Topeka, imagine the Executive refusing to enforce the law because it disagreed with the Supreme Court's Ruling. What would describe such a system?

The current system also allows the Executive and Legislative Branches of government to influence the selection of judges and justices, imposing a specific ideology that the courts and judges are expected to reflect rather than the law. As a result, there are certain prevailing viewpoints that nominees must express during the selection process, which determine whether a jurist is confirmed or not. Under similar methods, the Senate can refuse to confirm judges without redress.

For example, in 2018, the United States Senate, controlled by Republicans (the opposition party), refused to confirm a Supreme Court nominee that a Democratic Party's president had nominated because they opposed the President.

In 2022, the Liberian Senate replicated this behavior in the Liberian system by refusing to confirm President George Weah's nominee to the Supreme Court because they opposed him. Their actions demonstrated a lack of clarity of thought and independence in behavior. Were their actions in favor of the country or themselves?

The proposed reorganized Judicial system releases the courts from executive management, establishes independent funding sources for the courts separate from the Executive Branch, and empowers the judiciary to appoint its own jurists. There will also be a unified court system, which will include the Traditional courts that are formalized and codified accordingly.

The courts--the Supreme Court, Circuit Court, Monthly and Probate Court, Tax Court, Magistrates, Justices of the Peace Court, Traffic Court, and Juvenile Court--will be reorganized into the following categories:

- The Supreme Court
- Appellate Courts and Other Specialized Courts
- County Courts - Circuit Courts
- District Courts - Magistrates

The Supreme Court

The Supreme Court will hear appeals related to constitutional issues and disputes between districts, counties, and branches of government. It will also manage the court system and have authority over the lower courts.

The Supreme Court will consist of 15 justices, one from each county, who will gather to elect the Chief Justice.

The current court has five justices appointed by the president, including the Chief Justice. After the reorganization, the Council on the Law, Constitution, Legal, and Judiciary System shall recommend justices, judges, and magistrates to the Chief Justice for appointments. The justices shall vote amongst themselves to select a Chief Justice.

Justices will also hire their own clerks and internal staff through their respective Human Resources Departments rather than through the president.

Appellate Courts and Other Specialized Courts

There will be three Appellate Courts, each comprising five judges. Each court will preside over five counties and have jurisdiction over all appeals, including those related to taxes. The Appellate Courts are designed to be active and engaging, responding promptly to appeals throughout the year.

- **The Western Appellate Court** will cover Lofa, Cape Mount, Bomi, Bong, and Gbarpolu counties.
- **The Central Appellate Court** will oversee appeals from Margibi, Montserrado, Grand Bassa, Nimba, and Rivercess counties.

- **The Eastern Appellate Court** will handle appeals from Grand Gedeh, Maryland, Sinoe, River Gee, and Grand Kru counties.
- Other specialized courts shall be arranged in the Western, Central, and Eastern Regions of the country to exercise jurisdiction over the following:
  - **Uniform Court of Military Justice**
  - **Residency, Immigration and Naturalization Court**

Transfers to the Judiciary

- Transfers the functions and responsibilities of the Board of Tax Appeals to the court system.

County Courts

County/Circuit Courts will have jurisdiction over criminal and civil cases, with one court in each county. The Criminal Court shall be responsible for adjudicating life and death sentences. They, rather than the president, will order the execution of convicts by hanging.

County Criminal Court A: This court shall handle first-degree felonies such as rape, kidnapping, murder, arson, corruption, embezzlement, drug offenses, and cases involving bodily harm or death. It shall impose death sentences and life sentences, with no options for clemency or pardon.

- **County Criminal Court B:** This court shall address second-degree felonies, including robbery, sexual assault, corruption, embezzlement, fraud, assault, manslaughter, possession of a controlled substance, and child molestation. It will mandate sentences and allow for clemency only after half of the sentence has been served.

- **County Criminal Court C:** This court will handle third-degree felonies, including involuntary manslaughter, bribery, burglary, and larceny. It imposes prison sentences and allows for clemency.

- **County Civil Court D:** This court will hear civil cases exceeding $1 million, involving labor, torts, breach of contract, equitable claims, and land disputes.

- **County Civil Court E:** This court handles civil cases involving labor, torts, taxes, breach of contract, equitable claims, and land disputes with a value of less than $1 million.

- **County Administrative Court F:** This court will handle county and district administrative cases, including government matters, elections, voting-related offenses, taxation, zoning, and other related issues.

- **County Civil Court G:** Deals with the monthly and probate court, estate, will, and business.

District Courts - Magistrates

District Courts will be established in each district to have jurisdiction over misdemeanor and ordinance cases within their respective districts.

- **District Court A:** Misdemeanors, embezzlement, theft, property offenses, property damage, fraud, forgery, bribery, and counterfeiting.

- **District Court B:** Domestic and family court deals with juvenile cases, divorce, wills, trusts, family issues, and marriages.

- **District Court C:** Debts, small claims under five hundred dollars, ordinances, zoning, property disputes, district administrative cases (Government), elections, voting-related offenses, taxations, levies, residency, zoning, etc.

- **District Court D**: Traffic courts deal with transportation law.

- **District Court F:** Settle disputes concerning rites, customs, and traditions using available tools and technologies. The Traditional courts currently operate outside the legal system.

*Justices, judges, and magistrates will appoint their own clerks and internal staff through their respective Human Resources Departments rather than through the president.

For a long time, the Chief Justice and justices in the United States did not pay taxes on their income, a practice that was also adopted in Liberia. However, when the law changed in the U.S., Liberia's law did not follow suit. Furthermore, Chief Justices earn a salary equivalent to that of the Vice President, as specified in the Judiciary Law - Title 17 - Liberian Code of Laws Revised, and don't pay taxes on their incomes. Therefore, the tax issue will be reviewed as part of the reform.

Chapter 10:
Mayoral Assembly Branch

The House of Representatives has become an elephant carcass, where every rascal, rogue, scoundrel, and noble is vying for seats to assemble and devour their portion. Running for a legislative seat is the biggest hustle in the country, next to running for the presidency. The most outrageous part is that those already occupying these elected positions lack scruples and are unrestrained by any principle or law in their pursuit of personal gain.

Each year, the allocations for senators and representatives exceed the budgets of the state's defense, health, and education sectors. Together, these 103 individuals consume more of the nation's budget than they contribute. Although lawmakers pass bills that grant themselves perks and financial rewards, no law has been enacted to benefit individual Liberians directly in similar ways. Yet, they are as ineffective and corrupt as legislators in other African countries.

Every Speaker of the House of Representatives and his minions work fewer hours in the capital and rarely visit their districts to receive instruction from the people they represent. Even the legislation they enact is contrary to the will of their people and the country's interests. Despite that, they are not held accountable to the public.

Over time, they have amassed so much power that their salaries exceed the earnings of the lowest-paid public workers by a hundredfold. Along with their luxury cars, perks, scratch cards, allowances, gasoline coupons, and generous retirement benefits, they have enacted more laws to protect and enrich themselves.

The People's Redemption Council accused the True Whig Party's legislature of similar misconduct in 1980 and executed some of their members for those allegations.

More than four decades later, the current legislature's behavior has become worse than that of those overthrown. There is an urgent need to reform the legislature's roles, functions, responsibilities, and costs to mitigate the damage it inflicts on the country's economic, social, and political life and to change the perception of public service in society.

Within the last two decades, the individuals whose living standards, income, and wealth appear to be improving astronomically are lawmakers. They, the presidents, high-ranking government officials, and foreigners, are the only four groups of individuals who enjoy the country while the rest of the people suffer.

The current constitution enables the legislators to roam freely, unencumbered by the people's demands and wishes. This lack of accountability also allows lawmakers to prioritize their interests over those of their districts. But, the incoming reform will alter those perspectives and strip them of those powers and authorities.

New House of Representatives

First, the reform will transform the current House of Representatives into a unicameral legislative system similar to those in Mauritius, Nebraska (USA), Sweden, and Senegal, and rename it the Mayoral Assembly Branch of Government.

In this system, members will vote based on the decisions approved by their districts rather than relying on their personal beliefs, feelings, or the directives of their political parties.

It will consist of mayors elected from each district to represent their people. The new title for these officials will be Mayor-Representative. Each district will determine its Mayoral-Representative pay and compensation out of the district's budget.

Most importantly, they shall not be immune to prosecution.

In previous chapters, the Senate's roles and functions — such as providing advice, oversight, consent, and consultation — were transferred to the Advisory Council branch of government, reformed and reorganized.

The Mayoral Representative Assembly

The capital shall serve as the headquarters of the Mayoral Assembly and convene for a vote quarterly.

Its members shall elect the Speaker of the Assembly as head of this body, whose power and authority shall be limited accordingly.

Mayors from different districts will gather once every quarter or six months for a fourteen-day session to vote on national legislation that their districts (the people) have already discussed, debated, and approved.

The Assembly shall be designed for reading, reconciling, and voting on bills, rather than debating, to ensure a comprehensive decision-making process.

A General Secretariat shall be created to hire staff, coordinate research, formulate legislation, manage voting processes, and oversee the Assembly's day-to-day operations, similar to what was created in the Advisory Council.

New Role, Responsibilities, and Functions of the
Representative Mayors

- Mayoral-Representatives will be elected to lead their districts in coordinating legislative activities and administering, managing, and providing daily services to their districts, following the roles and responsibilities outlined in Chapter 3, Structures of The New State.

- Mayors will be required to live and work in their districts. They will serve their constituents by addressing their needs and concerns through community and town hall meetings, as well as utilizing the instruments of levies, propositions, and petitions to get things done. However, they will not have the power to create bills themselves. Like other residents, they must lobby their fellow citizens to support their proposals to have these bills enacted into law at the district level.

Reformed and Transferred Responsibilities and
Functions of Legislating

Declaration of New Districts and Cities: The boundaries of the districts have already been established and discussed in Chapter 3, which deals with the Structure of the State. This process eliminates gerrymandering and the need for the Mayoral Assembly to create or approve new counties and other political subdivisions.

Budgetary Appropriations: Budgetary appropriations within the national budget will be determined by percentages outlined in the Constitution and law. Every expenditure and revenue will be allocated based on these percentages to prevent the President and the mayors from altering, debating, or passing any aspect of national funding. These allocations will be enacted through referendums, enforced by the Central Bank, and reviewed quarterly and annually to ensure a stable and predictable budgetary process.

Taxes, Fines, Tariffs and Duties: ministries, agencies, county and district governments will establish and impose Taxes, fines, tariffs and duties. Each entity will have the authority to levy fines and fees for goods and services within its jurisdiction, which the Central Bank's Branches will enforce in accordance with the country's fiscal and economic policies.

Negotiation and Regulation: Ministries and institutions will negotiate and regulate trade and commerce between Liberia and other nations. However, these activities must be sanctioned or ratified by the Central Bank and Advisory Council and require public approval before being voted on or adopted into law by the Assembly of Mayors at the national level.

Entities at the district, county, ministerial, and institutional levels will have the authority to establish their own rules, regulations, and procedures governing the management and operations of their respective organizations, overseen by the Advisory Council.

To prevent the possibility of bribery or corruption, mayors shall be prohibited from altering a bill or voting against the consensus of their district at the Mayoral Assembly.

District Lawmaking

A proposed ordinance can originate from a community meeting and be voted on throughout or at the district meeting, where each community can vote to enact it into law. If a majority of communities within a district support the ordinance, it becomes law for that district. The district will enforce this local law as long as it does not violate the Constitution.

The people will use the same process to call for amendments, demand repeals of any act, recall and impeach elected officials, and register their vote of confidence.

In this framework, mayor-representatives will not hold more power than ordinary citizens. Every resident's vote will be equal, with each person entitled to one vote.

A Mayoral-Representative cannot legislate, vote against their district's will, or veto bills contrary to the people's votes. Before any international agreement, treaty, constitutional amendment, statute, or referendum is enacted, the people's verdict is required, and their mayor-representatives must adhere to the vote results.

When the majority of districts in a county adopt a law, it becomes county law. Similarly, when most districts in the country pass a law, it becomes a national law.

Before any proposal or bill is introduced for debate and vote, it must include the cost, source of funding, pros and cons, and net benefits to the people, district, or nation. Furthermore, it should accompany expert testimony and deliberations involving the departments responsible for implementing the bill.

National laws, statutes, constitutional acts, and referendums must also undergo review by the Advisory Council and undergo audits by the Central Bank before being enacted into law, and they must gain the people's approval.

Legislating

After campaigns, public discussions, research, debates, and efforts to raise awareness, a proposed bill or ordinance must receive at least 50% support from neighborhoods before it can be sent to the Election Commission for a districtwide vote. The exact process will be used to approve laws at the county and national levels.

This form of direct democracy will be adapted so that districts instruct and restrict their mayoral-representatives and national leaders to vote only on the positions they approve. A similar approach will be adopted for districts and counties enacting levies and borrowing, as well as Liberia's stance on international treaties, agreements, and conventions, where applicable.

Elections and District Voting System

The district voting system will be set up using a combination of the diagrammatic and demographic models used by the Special Emergency Life Food Program and the Ebola mapping system. These statistical systems were used to distribute food in Monrovia and identify victims nationwide during the Ebola crisis.

Mobile money applications and their security features have also helped refine measures and optimize valuable deployment targets, enabling them to be made electronically secure and credible. Combined, the system will be developed and used for voting and outreach in the country.

When candidates are approved for elections, their ballots will be distributed through the voting system for each district, or may be restricted to a specific district where residents are eligible to vote. Individuals registered outside of that geographic area will not receive a ticket and will not be allowed to vote.

This system will enable each district to accurately determine the number of voters who participated within its boundaries and ensure precise tabulation of the results.

The system will also ensure that districts conduct voting liberally and that problems arising from that formulation are also resolved at the district level.

The voting system shall be electronic and secure to ensure the integrity of elections and voting organized by districts.

Residents within Liberia and abroad will be able to vote remotely in their respective districts. Furthermore, voting results will be announced minutes or an hour after the polls close.

Further measures will be devised to outlaw the financing of elections and campaigns by foreign nations and organizations, and to prevent external influences, thereby rendering the involvement of foreign observers unnecessary and potentially illegal.

Campaign Reform

Campaigning will be restructured and strictly regulated to prevent local and national candidates from using international media to solicit external influence and interference, such as foreign funding or intervention, as has been the case in the past.

The new law will impose limits on certain political activities, especially those involving media engagement, promotion, campaign financing, and timelines. Violators will be fined or expelled from the process. The paramount importance of such a law is safeguarding the nation's sovereignty and ensuring independence over the country's elections, campaigning, and voting processes.

General Reform Policies

1. Fiscal and Public Financial Management Reform

The Fiscal and Public Financial Management Reform Act seeks to reform taxes, expenditures, revenue, the budget, and debt, including regulatory, accounting, and management processes.

The new act will operate in the realms of growth, development, efficiency, transparency, and accountability.

The act will reform fiscal policy in line with the restructuring and consolidation of ministries and agencies. Reassess taxes and the tax system and address expenditures, revenues, credit, and debt.

It will also classify funds disbursed to districts, defense, national security, law enforcement, health, education, and cash transfers as mandatory spending.

The county's and districts' finances will be handled and managed separately and independently from the national government.

For instance, the Resident Tax system, designed to ensure local autonomy and the efficient allocation of resources, shall be exclusively collected and reserved by districts to fund local services and development. This management strategy will apply similarly to other branches of government, ministries, and agencies.

Every revenue a ministry or agency generates shall be deposited directly into that ministry's or institution's account, not into a General Account.

All revenues and expenses shall be debited and credited against the corresponding accounts.

As these ministries and institutions operate on a basis of a balanced budget, if they spend above the threshold of the revenues raised, the Central Bank will distribute the remaining funds, and they shall repay the Central Bank with interest. But, if they operate in a manner that generates surpluses, they will be rewarded with the opportunity to use the extra funds to distribute staff bonuses, increase pay, or upgrade their equipment and offices.

The Central Bank will be responsible for implementing and enforcing these reforms, including fiscal and budgetary discipline.

The Advisory Council on Banking, Finance, Taxes, Business, Employment, Competitive Advantage, and Investments will oversee public finance and the country's central banking system to ensure these policies align with the reform's objectives, which ultimately benefit the State and its people.

2. Defense, National Security, and Police Reform

The Act is intended to establish a robust framework for defense, security, and law enforcement to safeguard the nation.

The reform will consolidate all the security and defense institutions and their funding to ensure the country is adequately defended.

It will also include the creation of the National Service Corps, as well as Defense, National Security, and Police Colleges, and provide funding for the construction of barracks, training bases, and arms and equipment to enhance operational readiness.

Everything, from training and psychology to uniforms, service, and pay, will be reformed.

The overarching goal is to prioritize Liberia's National Defense, Security, and Law Enforcement interests above all, not those of an individual or a president, and to bring more honor and pride to the men and women who serve the country.

The Ministry of Defense, National Security, and Police will implement these reforms and enforce this policy, with their actions overseen by the Council on Defense, National Security, and Police.

3. State and Foreign Affairs Reform

The State and Foreign Affairs Reform Act will prioritize two key areas: regulations and law enforcement related to national issues, and the management of international relations through the Foreign Affairs Division.

This reform involves the merger and consolidation of national and foreign policies, operations, and functions under a single institution.

The Ministry of State and Foreign Affairs will implement these reforms and enforce this policy, while the Council of State oversees them.

4. Medical and Public Health Reform

The Medical and Public Health Reform aims to provide funding for healthcare through an insurance scheme where patients pay for the care and services they receive.

The reform focuses on both curative and preventive medicine, improving accessibility for all and promoting a patient-centered system.

A key aspect of this reform is the transfer of ownership of former government healthcare facilities to medical professional corporations owned by Liberians.

Under the reform, regulatory bodies will establish and implement health policies. The Ministry of Health, a key player, will oversee its enforcement, ensuring the reform's effective implementation. Accrediting agencies will also play a crucial role in evaluating and licensing medical professionals and institutions to uphold high standards.

The Council on Health, Education, and Skills Development will play a pivotal role in overseeing the implementation of these reforms, providing reassurance about the coordination of healthcare improvement in Liberia.

5. Education and Human Development Reform

This Act will introduce an innovative education voucher system, which provides tuition funding for each student and gives pupils and their parents the freedom to choose their preferred schools.

This reform proposes better learning environments and promotes competition and choice within the education sector, where public learning institutions are transferred to private owners.

It also fosters a supportive higher education environment that cultivates a smart, capable society, where students are locally trained to apply their knowledge and skills to address problems within their districts.

The Ministry of Education and other relevant agencies will play a crucial role in this reform by providing planning, regulations, and enforcement to ensure the smooth and effective implementation of the new education system.

The Council on Health, Education, and Skills Development will oversee the implementation of the reform.

6. National Fuel and Energy Reform

The National Oil Company of Liberia will undergo reforms and restructuring to become the National Oil and Energy Company, taking responsibility for the national fuel, energy supply, and power distribution networks.

This initiative aims to construct and maintain energy infrastructure and reserve channels to address energy and fuel shortages, meet rising demand, and stabilize fluctuating prices.

The National Oil Company will ensure that the country has sufficient fuel and energy to power homes, factories, farms, businesses, industries, and development activities.

The Council on Land, Forest, Water, Energy, Power, Reserves, Natural Resources, Environment, and Hygiene will oversee the institutions and agencies responsible for implementing and enforcing these reforms.

7. Natural Mineral Reserves Reform

The Central Bank will create and manage the National Natural Mineral Reserves Account, focusing on strategic minerals such as gold, diamonds, lithium, uranium, timber, and cobalt.

The target for each mineral shall be set at a minimum of $10 billion.

The Council on Land, Forest, Water, Energy, Power, Reserves and Natural Resources, Environment, and Hygiene will oversee the reforms in these sectors.

8. National Infrastructure, Transportation, & Communication Network Reform

The Act will outline plans, funding, and designs for the construction and improvement of roads, buildings, transportation systems, and communication and electrical networks.

These plans will include clear timelines, budgets, and steps to ensure that the work is of high quality and built to last.

The Armed Forces of Liberia, rather than foreign entities, will be responsible for designing the country's strategic and comprehensive development and infrastructure plans. They will also carry out the construction.

Oversight of institutions, ministries, and agencies engaged in this reform process shall be the responsibility of the Advisory Council on National Planning, Buildings, Infrastructure, and Network Development rather than the president.

9. Food and Self-Sufficiency Reform

The Food and Self-Sufficiency Act aims to grow, manage, and coordinate food and agricultural activities to meet at least 80% of Liberia's domestic food needs.

This will be achieved through the following initiatives: Funding agricultural colleges through scholarships and the Center for Agricultural Research Institute (CARI) to provide the scientific training, techniques, and skills necessary for advanced farming.

Invest in large-scale food producers, corporations, technologies, and agricultural activities through the Central Bank, ensuring the country's staple foods and livestock are produced efficiently.

Each county will prioritize the production of at least ten of the top crops or foods that Liberians consume, aiming for 80% local production before starting any exports.

Strengthen the manufacturing sector to process foods for both local and export markets.

The Ministry of Agriculture, along with other regulatory bodies, will implement reforms focusing on food production, distribution, cost, security, and safety.

The Agriculture, Food, and Industry Advisory Council will oversee their activities to prevent sudden policy changes and to ensure consistent practices.

10. Conservation and Environmental Reform

The Conservation and Environmental Reform will prioritize reforestation, land protection, wetland management, and wildlife conservation, invest in Ecological Tourism, and ban logging exports.

This initiative will regulate or prohibit mining, farming, hunting, local logging, and fishing activities within national parks and reserves, aiming to ensure the responsible management of land, water, and air to safeguard the country's vegetation, wildlife, and forests.

Local communities and districts will receive training on environmental stewardship and enforcement. For instance, how to maintain the grass over the land to prevent erosion and fine those who refuse or fail to do so.

Additionally, the reform will reevaluate building materials, construction techniques, and technologies, adopting methods that address pollution, manage flooding, and prevent erosion.

The Council on Land, Forest, Water, Energy, Power, Reserves, Environment, and Hygiene will oversee the agencies and institutions responsible for implementing and enforcing this policy.

11. Crimes and Enforcement Reform

The Crimes and Enforcement Reform seeks to enforce tough sentences and severe penalties for criminal violations, misdemeanors, and infringements, including substantial fines, life imprisonment, and the death penalty.

This reform will establish systems and processes to ensure proper training, discipline, and compensation for police and law enforcers.

Law enforcement and crime punishment will be reorganized and divided into two categories: county and district.

The courts in counties will focus on national law, while the district courts deal with local cases.

County law enforcement will operate under the county government, guided by a board responsible for recruiting officers and overseeing investigations and disciplinary actions.

Death row and long-term inmates will serve time in county correctional facilities, where they will contribute labor for national and county projects.

At the district level, law enforcement will be under the Jurisdiction of the District Governments.

District leaders and the board are responsible for recruiting officers and managing police activities. Each district will maintain at least one police detachment with a jail to enhance law enforcement and ensure public safety.

All these institutions and agencies shall be overseen by the Council of State and the Council on the Law, Constitution, Legal, Elections, and Judiciary System, and the Council on Defense, National Security, and Police.

12. Legal Representation Reform

This Act will offer funding for individuals accused or charged in criminal cases, allowing them to use vouchers to hire private legal representation. This initiative ensures that everyone has equal access to evidence, skilled attorneys, and legal representation.

The State will no longer appoint public defenders. Instead, all parties involved -- the State, the prosecution, and the accused -- must hire their own attorneys to ensure fairness and impartiality.

Both the accused and the defendants will have equal access to evidence gathered by law enforcement and investigators.

The council leading the oversight of the institutions, ministries, and agencies involved in these reforms shall be the Council on the Law, Constitution, Legal, and Judiciary System.

13. Stricter Sentencing Guidelines Reform

The Stricter Sentencing Guidelines Reform Act will establish severe penalties, including life sentences and fines for felonies and misdemeanors.

The Act will impose the death penalty for serious offenses such as murder, ritualistic murder, rape, drug trafficking, and public corruption involving amounts over one million dollars.

The Council on the Law, Constitution, Legal and Judiciary System shall oversee these reforms and their institutions and agencies.

14. Drug Policy Reform

Marijuana and alcohol will be legalized but subjected to higher taxation. All other recreational drugs will remain illegal and will be subject to confiscation and prosecution.

Under the new law, drug kingpins and public officials involved in these offenses will face the death penalty.

Three councils will oversee the entities and institutions implementing the reforms: the Council on the Law, Constitution, Legal System, and Judiciary, and the Council of State and the Council on Defense, National Security, and Police.

15. Disasters and Emergency Relief Reform

The National Service Corps will conduct disaster relief efforts nationwide. This includes aiding individuals impacted by disasters, managing emergencies, and supporting recovery efforts under the Disaster and Emergency Relief Reform Act.

The Council on Welfare, Relief, and Public Service will oversee the reforms in this area.

16. Wealth Creation Policy Act

The Wealth Creation Policy Act aims to promote economic prosperity and ensure financial security for individuals, families, and businesses. Its goals include making sure that income covers the basic living expenses of the average citizen and keeps pace with the cost of living. Additionally, the Act seeks to ensure that Liberians hold a majority of shares in corporate stocks and ownership.

Key provisions of the act include:

- Disbursing cash transfers to individuals who meet specific legal and financial criteria.

- Creating and enforcing laws to penalize the government and employers who fail to promptly and accurately compensate workers.

- Establishing a Homestead Act to provide land to millions, protect land ownership, and facilitate home building.

- Adopting a low-tax economic model to reduce income taxes and eliminate taxes on dividends, capital gains, and estate and inheritance taxes.

- Lower corporate tax rates, reduce interest rates, increase liquidity for businesses and entrepreneurs, and simplify the business startup process and regulatory operations.

The Council on Banking, Finance, Taxes, Business, Employment, Insurance, Investments, and Competitive Advantage will lead the reforms in Wealth Creation.

17. Industrialization and Trade Policy

Previous governments in Liberia heavily relied on foreign investments for industrialization and trade, which left many Liberians with limited opportunities to pursue small businesses through the Liberianization Policy.

The Industrialization and Trade Reform aims to give the Central Bank control over specific key industries, reserving them for Liberian-led corporations and firms. This initiative seeks to promote greater economic independence, security, and self-reliance.

The goal of this policy is to create large corporations that can create jobs, boost wealth creation, and produce goods and services for local consumption and use. By empowering Liberian corporations to compete effectively in local and regional markets, these companies will be able to offer competitive products and services at affordable prices. Additionally, the policy will impose restrictions on specific minerals and sectors, prohibiting foreign investment and participation in these areas.

The plan includes the establishment and funding of over 67 key privatized national corporations to meet market demands and support exports.

The Council on Commerce, Tariffs, Industries, Trade, Imports, and Exports will oversee the development and enforcement of these industries.

18. Governance Policy Reform

The Council of State on Regulation, National, County and District Affairs, and Executive Powers and Authority, shall oversee the country's Governance Policy Reform Act and serve as the country's governing Board of Directors.

This act ensures adherence to governance principles, upholds the rule of law, and defends the sovereignty of the State under the Council's guidance.

Under this act, the Council will interview and recommend public officials for appointments and elections, among other responsibilities. Have access to national defense and security information on par with that of the president and govern in the president's absence. They will manage transitions during elections and serve as a last resort for addressing all state issues.

This model draws inspiration from governance systems used in Iran, Switzerland, Singapore, Cuba, and China.

19. Residency and Immigration Reform

The Residency and Immigration Reform Act will establish requirements for everyone living in the country to declare and maintain a residency status. This status will grant individuals, citizens, and foreigners the rights and privileges to live, work, and vote within their districts.

The Act also aims to manage the entry and stay of foreigners within the country. It will include various programs, opportunities, and strategies to protect and defend the nation, as well as encourage and support Liberians abroad to return home. These reforms will also attract and recruit a talented workforce from around the world, as well as individuals who wish to live and raise their families in Liberia.

The Council of State on Regulation, National, County, and District Affairs, and Executive Powers and Authority will oversee the reform in these areas.

20. Elections and Voting Reforms

The Council on Law, Constitution, Legal Affairs, Elections, and the Judiciary will oversee the Elections and Voting Reform Act, which mandates compulsory voting for all individuals aged 16 and older. Establish age limits for running for elected office and serving in elected positions.

This law will outline the structure and operation of elections, eligibility, financing, campaigning, voter education, debates, and forums.

In addition to organizing and conducting elections at the district level, the new law shall require that all ballots be cast electronically. This includes all residents of the country, including foreigners and Liberians living abroad.

Everyone will have the opportunity to vote on propositions, levies, and the election of town chiefs, community presidents, and mayor-representatives. Only citizens living in the country shall be eligible to vote for the President and candidates to the Advisory Council.

21. Accountability, Pay, and Compensation Reform

The Council on Banking, Finance, Taxes, Business, Employment, Insurance, Investments, and Competitive Advantage will lead the oversight of institutions and ministries implementing the reform of the Accountability, Pay, and Compensation Reform Act.

The new law will require all (public) corporations, ministries, and employers to disclose their financial statements on their websites, including details on staff numbers, job descriptions, salaries, benefits, and overall compensation.

The Central Bank, the Ministry of Labor and Justice, and other relevant regulators will be responsible for establishing a transparent pay and compensation system and structures.

22. Math, Science, Engineering, Technology, and Innovation Reform

This Reform Act aims to invest in STEM fields through partnerships with universities, corporations, schools, and technology service centers, making these disciplines and services accessible and attractive to everyone, and giving Liberia a competitive advantage in STEM.

The act will include programs that provide training, scholarships, and externships, as well as recognizing outstanding achievements in STEM with national awards and cash prizes.

Provisions within the law will also provide microgrants through district banks to support the development of promising local technology hubs, innovations, products, and services, as facilitated by the Central Bank.

To attract talent in the field, the Act will ensure competitive pay and salaries for STEM jobs and offer subsidies and complementary tax incentives for corporations and institutions involved in the field.

The Council on Science, Technologies, and Inventions shall oversee the institutions and ministries implementing these reforms.

23. Media and Communication Policy Reform

The Council on Media, Culture, Religion, Tourism, Sports, Gaming, Traditions, and Customs will be responsible for overseeing the institutions and agencies that are responsible for reforming and managing media and communication in the country.

This initiative aims to restrict ownership of media institutions and gaming operations to Liberians and protect their operations.

All public institutions and agencies will be mandated to establish their own press offices and websites to disseminate information and communicate with the public.

The law will protect press freedom by making it illegal for the government and public officials to shut down media organizations.

It also imposes penalties for violations of this freedom, including prosecuting any damage to media institutions and physical harm inflicted on journalists or reporters as a second-degree felony.

Conversely, there will be huge fines and prison sentences imposed on individuals and institutions that engage in the behavior of spreading aspersion and disinformation.

Take steps to make activities related to culture, tourism, and sports robust and impactful—launch initiatives to enhance the country's image. Help reform museums, libraries, and the arts; produce books, music, films, and other forms of art, aligning these efforts with the country's vision and reform initiatives.

Privatized the management of teams, competitions, sports venues, and services by Liberian owners, athletes, and investors across the nation.

Impose taxes on religious and faith-based institutions, assets, and activities at the district and national levels. And ensure that they treat Liberians with respect and dignity, and refrain from engaging in activities that lower the quality of life for members.

Conclusion

Reform is written to help Liberia restructure and reform itself to achieve political stability, ensure its own defense, grow its economy, provide opportunities, and create wealth. The book aims to inspire change, improve living standards, and rebuild Liberia.

The ideas in the book are also intended to assist other developing nations, such as Haiti and Somalia, in properly reforming and rebuilding their countries, rather than relying solely on the ideas of a president and a political party. The proposed system is also designed to be immune to overthrows. These ideas and concepts even make places like Rwanda, Burkina Faso, and El Salvador, which are thriving under strong patriotic presidents, more resilient.

Unlike reforms that have occurred through the actions of dictators, violence, and the IMF, as was the case in Ghana under Jerry Rawlings, the new type of change comes from the people, not even the government.

The book proposes a concept that establishes robust structures and systems that can easily adapt to changing policies, dictated by the people, rather than the old system that has easily obliterated governments, systems, presidents, or policies in Africa, as have occurred in Liberia, Sudan, and Libya. Second, the new systems enable people to collectively discuss, evaluate, and scrutinize policies before they are implemented, rather than having them imposed upon them.

Many people in the developing world have viewed democracy in their countries as a replacement for colonial rule. Their leaders tell them what they should have or do, just as the colonists did. Hence, for Liberians and other Africans who do not view the imported democracy as a viable means of governance to achieve the desired changes in their respective countries, the ideas and concepts presented in this book serve as that antidote.

This impetus to initiate change locally enables people to envision the kind of future and quality of life they aspire to for their nations, themselves, and future generations. It helps them to reassess the purpose of their nations and tie it into the structures of their country, government, and institutions. It reflects how citizens are empowered to make decisions about what they want and instruct both their presidents and governments to work within the confines of their dictates.

Liberia has remained stagnant, maintaining the status quo before the publication of this book. However, it can no longer be unclear about which direction to take. The opportunity to reposition and transform itself into something remarkable, like Singapore, is NOW within reach. Change has come to Liberia, and for Liberians everywhere, regardless of their education, wealth, class, or connections.

Change is coming to hundreds of millions of young, vibrant, and energetic people across Africa as well, who are hungry and roaming the streets of their cities in search of food, and have no idea where their next meal will come from.

Change is on its way to those confined to poverty, illiteracy, and ravaged by disease, who are wondering how a change in their circumstances will arise.

To you who are also dealing with dictatorship and the fixtures of everlasting presidents, and whose country's economic and political situation is dire, and are leaving to seek survival and opportunities abroad as the only alternative. Change has come for you, too.

No longer can your countries and leaders be uncertain about the path they pursue, or shift the responsibility for improving your living standards onto foreigners within Africa—the reform needed to solve those problems, improve lives, and achieve greatness is within everyone's reach. How well you induce change will be up to you.

As powerful nations around the world shift and realign, there is minimal room for countries that remain bifurcated and indecisive. In today's global landscape, every nation and its people must make their voices heard, take bold stances, and clarify their positions, just as El Salvador, Rwanda, Cuba, Mali, and Burkina Faso have done. Such clarity of purpose enables a nation to stand out, endure, and thrive. That is the opportunity this book offers every third-world nation and its people.

Making these ideas and concepts of change and systems possible, enforceable, and sustainable relies on the collective rather than the individual. It protects capable leaders in developing countries and prevents any attempts to remove or overthrow them and change their ideas.

In this system, when a country adopts this approach, even the deaths of its leaders, as was the case with John Magufuli of Tanzania and Muammar Gaddafi of Libya, won't change the trajectory of the country. It is similar to structures and systems in Sweden, Iran, Cuba, China, and Singapore, which have made it impossible to coerce or compromise their leaders into pursuing goals and objectives that contradict national interests or sovereignty.

Without such a system in places like Rwanda, Burkina Faso, Russia, Mali, and Niger, the reforms achieved in the last decades are likely to be reversed after their nationalistic leaders have left the stage.

New leaders can undo their progress with fake or weak reforms, just as happened with Thomas Sankara and Blaise Compaoré in Burkina Faso, and with Luiz Inácio Lula da Silva and Jair Bolsonaro in Brazil.

The proposed structures and systems, accompanied by a National Plan, not only sustain a country but also continue the policies and legacies of their former great leaders, as succeeding administrations have done in China, Singapore, and Cuba.

As you eagerly anticipate the message of Reform in Liberia and across Africa, remember, it's the reforms individual nations pursue that will make the difference. Liberia, with its potential, can be the beacon that guides the rest of Africa. Africa may not speak with one voice today, but the individual reforms and resilience that take hold will surely make the continent a force to reckon with.

Bookcover designed by **Ace Sadler-Esp.**

www.ingramcontent.com/pod-product-compliance
Lightning Source LLC
Chambersburg PA
CBHW051138120626
46547CB00012B/857